The
Butterfly
Fields

The Butterfly Fields

A Journey of Spiritual Healing and Enlightenment

CAROLE VICKIE PILCHER

authorHOUSE®

AuthorHouse™
1663 Liberty Drive
Bloomington, IN 47403
www.authorhouse.com
Phone: 1-800-839-8640

First published by AuthorHouse   02/14/2012

ISBN: 978-1-4678-8518-8 (sc)
ISBN: 978-1-4678-8519-5 (ebk)

Printed in the United States of America

CONTENTS

Foreword xi

Introduction xiii

Acknowledgements xv

The Seed of Life 1

My family 3

Life 7

Ordinary 9

Journey 11

Forgiveness 14

What Do You See? 17

Alone 19

The Darkness 22

Think 24

For My Friend 27

Protector 28

Admiration 30

Rain 32

Sometimes 34

Wealth 36

Ray of Light 38

The River 43

Waterfall 46

Be Free 49

Children 55

Sitting By a Candle 60

Time to BE 64

Cry 68

Dreams 71

The Beautiful Dream 72

My Best Friend 75

My Angel 78

For You, My Son 80

Nature 85

The Butterfly Fields 87

Counting Blessings 88

Spirit World 89

I am 93

Destiny 95

Children of Light 97

The Rainbow Bridge 99

Drums 101

Angel Embrace 103

Special Place 106

Healing 108

Going Home 109

Touching the Earth 110

Make You Think 113

Tick Tock 116

I See 119

The Tree 121

Saying Goodbye 125

The Good as Well as the Bad 127

Weakness 130

What Would You Do? 132

Friends 136

Address the Balance 138

The Mist 142

Feeling Low 145

The Road We Travel 147

Plough the field 150
The Power of Thought 152
My Craggy Tree 153
What is Happening to the World Today? 156
Love 158
Hope 159
All in a Day 161
Just For You 165
Change 168
Freedom 171
Christmas Seed 175
Moving On 177

Epilogue 181

For Mum and Dad

Without you I would not be the person I am today,

I was yesterday or will be tomorrow.

Much love to you both always.

FOREWORD

By Olga Levancuka

Carole's poems are stories. They are beautiful stories, of one human being who is going through life as each of us do on a daily basis, bringing our attention to our family, life, relationships and other situations we have no choice but to live.

As you read them, they give you this shiver of emotions, *your* emotions, sweeping through your body, as though they've been allowed to come out at last and to be treasured. Those emotions, you re-live as you read each poem, suddenly fill you with new light and understanding of them and leaving you feeling somewhat lighter.

If you ever thought your life is banal or coarse, Carole shows you the beautiful side of seemingly ordinary if not painful situations. It is almost as though she un-wraps your own emotions you experience and feel during similar events and then she serves them to you on that fluffy white cloud with the golden trim and it is spiced up with love and care.

At times we just want empathy. Yet even more, we want sympathy. Yes, we want to have the reassurance that the experiences, no matter how painful or possibly pleasurable, are ok. We want to be sure that there is another human being who has gone through that and at the end of those events, has become even better, happier and richer.

Carole's poems are definitely healing. There is just nothing else I've ever experienced as the emotions flowing over me as I read her poems.

Read her book and you'll know what I mean. It is not possible to describe that connection you go through on many levels. You will extract the bits which make you sad, make you happy or possibly even inspire. Her poems are your friends you can turn to at any time you feel as talking to.

I suggest you keep it as your diary and turn to it at times you feel you want to have that conversation with someone who *understands* you. Just as I do.

Thank you Carole for such an amazing gift to all of us,

Olga Levancuka,
Author of controversial "How to be Selfish (And other uncomfortable advice)." book.

INTRODUCTION

Hi I'm Carole and I would like to invite you to join me in what has been my journey through life thus far.

I was born in a small village in Kent and still live close to where I grew up with my parents and older brother. Being a parent to my two teenage children has been the most wonderful (and difficult) experience. It is a true privilege to be mum to two wonderfully gifted individuals who light up my life in so many ways.

Many things in my life have been challenging, the most being my disability. Looking physically different than other people has been something I have had to come to terms with along with the discrimination, isolation and emotional heartache that comes with it. The lessons I have learned throughout the years have been painful, sometimes I wondered if it was possible to ever feel whole, to love myself in any way at all. But my inner strength has been my driving force and realizing Spirit and allowing them into my life has enabled me to come to terms with and accept myself.

I have had a love of writing from a very young age. My profound love of books is well known to my friends and family, and one day I felt inspired to pick up a pen and write my very first poem; *Journey.*

From that day it seemed that poetry has become my emotional outlet and I am now often found with pen in hand and scribbling down my innermost thoughts. My favourite place is a field near to where I live and at certain times of the year it is awash with the most beautiful butterflies, much of my inspiration I have found in this very tranquil place, so close to nature.

From my very darkest days to days when I feel great joy in my life, it all goes down on paper, the trials of everyday life to questions that I may have whirling around my head and no answer to. I find that along with my trusty pen and note pad Spirit are ever present, wanting to jump in and have their say at any given opportunity.

They have been ever present through my hardest of challenges, helped guide me through serious illness and relationship turmoil. Helping me to understand that love and forgiveness should be part of who we are and what we practice on a daily basis.

Healing of others has been integral to my own healing journey, I am a practicing Spiritual Healer, Crystal Healer and I am studying Colour Therapy. Helping others to heal themselves enabling them to see their true pathway and their own inner light is a privilege and something I hold dear to my heart.

I am sure that as you yourself take your very own journey through life there will be days of darkness and light, great happiness and days tinged with sadness. In the pages of this book you will find upliftment and enlightenment, helping you see that life is indeed beautiful, filled with highs and lows, lessons to be learnt and that we are all Spiritual beings here to help and guide one another.

The real beauty of poetry is that it can be your constant companion, you can read a poem as many times as you wish, take what you wish from it then come back another day open another page and take another journey. I hope you enjoy reading *The Butterfly Fields* as much as I enjoyed writing it.

Love & Light
Carole

ACKNOWLEDGEMENTS

There are many people who I would like to express much gratitude toward who have made it possible for me to believe in myself and get my work in a book at last . . .

Firstly I would like to thank Spirit, my constant companions through the good and the bad, helping me step out from the darkness and providing such inspiration.

Mum & Dad, for everything, for making me the person I am today, for your utter unshakeable belief in everything I have ever done throughout my life. Words will never be adequate . . .

My beautiful children, Tom & Jordy, you are my everything. Your beautiful light keeps me from stumbling around in the darkness. Thank you for your love and patience in the hours I worked to put this book together

Thank you to Olga Levancuka, for your guidance, support and beautiful words.

To all at Westerham Spiritualist Centre, you know exactly who you are. You're words of encouragement and love have meant more than you could ever know. From the first time I ever got up and read out my first poem until now, the road seems to have been long but at last here we are!

To all my friends, the many times you have proof read my work, for your love and your support.

Sharon, for picking me up every time I fall down and making sense of it all, my best friend, my Soul Mate.

To Shane, thank you for supplying your wonderful pictures in this book. May you're future be bright.

Last but certainly not least my beautiful friend and Mentor Robbie Gant. Without your steadfast support, encouragement and complete unwavering faith in me I truly think this book would have been a lot longer in the making, if ever. You're words of wisdom help me to understand not just who I am, but where I am heading and how to get there. Your Spiritual light shines so brightly my friend and I am truly blessed to be part of your life. Thank you for the laughter you, never ever fail to make me smile. Much love x

(All images within this book are ©Shane Turnbull)

Looking back will make you wish you had

Looking forward will make you realize you can

The Seed of Life

Life can be a curious thing
Many strange things it can bring
Whether that be something beautiful happening to you
Maybe for once *your* foot fits the Prince's shoe
Or dark and troubled times
Situations that get us into a bind
Everything that we experience, touch and hold
Has the ability to bring us in from the cold
You see my friends, you must remember this
In every turn and every twist
Life is sown from the tiniest seed
Don't dismiss even the most humble weed
Beauty often comes from within
Open your ears, separate the music from the din
Everywhere we go we scatter new seeds
Be it from spoken word or physical deeds
It doesn't matter who, when, what or where
So long as they are scattered with infinite care
Hold onto this alone, in times of strife
You; my friends all have within you the Seed of Life . . .

Seed of life
© Shane Turnbull

My family

My family as I have discovered is extensive
I have spent many hours alone, being pensive
Thinking about my life thus far
And how often I have wished upon a falling star

In my darkest hour is where I have truly found
The family who I can count on who have always gathered round
When my heart has been hard and cold
It is my family who has bought me back into the fold

My darling children, my angels from above
Day after day you wrap me up in your glorious love
Making the battles seem easier to face
If I know I will always see your beautiful smiling grace

Tom, you are so very strong
And always sing your own song
I have learnt many lessons from you
Your heart will always be true

Your love for everything shines from your eyes
You always encourage me to climb my stiles
Holding my hand when I don't know what to do
Making me laugh when I feel blue

Jordy, you have grown into a beautiful swan
And like your brother you will always sing your own song
Your individuality makes you the person you are
Carry on with that and it will take you far

But your soul is something to behold
You have the ability to show such warmth, banishing the cold
When it counts and the chips are down
You are always there ready to help erase my worried frown

My mum is a beautiful person indeed
With her I can be myself, there is no need
For me to behave in a certain way
Always by my side, listening to what I need to say

Offering words of advice to help me see
Never ignoring my desperate pleas
The love she has shown me shines like the sun
She is amazing, she is my wonderful mum

There is my dad, how silly is he?
He has taught me about the person I need to be
My courage and drive to never give up come what may
To listen to myself, not to what others say

He has made me laugh from the day I arrived
An essential mix with love, helping me to thrive
He has been the tower of strength as I grew
Along with mum he helped me to myself to be true

My brother to whom I send such love
I will always be here my beautiful bruv
As children I think we shared a common ground
But as I grew strong, you became lost, impossible to be found

However there was a time when you heard my call
Even if you don't know it you never let me fall
When my world fell apart that day
You helped me even though it was for a short while you stayed

My beautiful, beautiful friend
I hope and pray we will journey till the end
You have seen me at my very worst
Always at the front of the queue to hold me first

Your compassion and love always reaching out
Never ever leaving me in any doubt
That you are my soul mate in so many ways
And I will treasure you every night and day

Then there is my dog, how could I forget
I am ever grateful for the day we met
Although you don't speak so others hear
I listen and understand when you are near

Your love for me shines from within
Loving me whatever, happy, sad, fat or thin
My angel sent from spirit to help me through
Oh my friend how I love you

Then I have to count all the others in my life
Who are always there through good times and trouble and strife
I have many people who I count as friends
Some come and go like passing trends

Others they have stuck around
My love for them and them for me keeps me on solid ground
I know that everyone around me evokes every kind of feeling
And that the love they show is amazingly healing

You see my family is around me wherever I am
You don't care if I look dowdy or glam
You will love me come what may
And never leave my side whatever I say

So this is my ode to all of you
You gave me wings and I flew
You helped me stand when I fell
You keep my secrets never to tell
You help me to walk when I want to run
You are there to share my laughter and fun
You dry my tears when I cry
You give me hope when mine dies

I count my blessings on a daily basis
That you always there, loving beautiful faces
Giving to me when you don't always know
You all make it possible for me to carry on with the show

Life

Life can be fun, life can be sweet
Life can be orderly and neat
Life can make us smile every day
Life can show us that there is another way
Life can be full of riches abound
Life can be hiding new adventures to be found
Life can generate such amazing acts of selfless love
Life can be touched often by Angels above
Life can show us that there is sometimes pain
Life will enable us from these situations to gain
Life will often put obstacles in our way
Life can leave us speechless, not much to say
Life will provide us with the tools we need
Life will give us opportunities to succeed
Life for some is full of adulation and fame
Life for others is full of hardship, nothing to gain
Life may not have turned out as planned
But for every hardship the stronger you stand
Take hold of every opportunity that knocks at your door
You never know what may lay in store
A new direction could be long overdue
Time for you to try something new
After all . . .
Life is funny, life is strange
Life has a way of turning a new page
Listen closely and watch with a keen eye
And you will understand that you have to try
For life is our very own lesson plan
And it is irrelevant if you stand alone or have an army of fans

For it is what you gain that matters most
Remaining true to your Soul to which this earthly body is your host
So when life becomes hard and your view is obscured
Remember life will present you with a cure
All you have to do is open your heart and mind
And life will present you with the answers you need to find

Ordinary

I am ordinary in every way
No matter what others may say
I am no different than you
I have nothing special, nothing new
I am ordinary in an extraordinary world
Often into impossible situations hurled
Once I am in the thick of it
Just like you I want to scream and hit
I am an ordinary person walking my path
Sometimes I cry, sometimes I laugh
But just like you my heart is filled with love
And as you I am watched over by Angels above
I am ordinary in the things that I do
Does it really matter if I am Catholic, Christian, Hindu or Jew?
Surely when I reach out to a friend in need
Whatever I practice I am sowing a positive seed
I am ordinary when I speak to my Guides
I have no reason to hide
I can be honest about my feelings
And ask for some much needed healing
I am ordinary, I feel fear
I have moments when I believe no one can hear
I am no stronger than the man next to me
Often I want to turn and flee
I am ordinary; I have no amazing, awesome power
Like you sometimes I need the strength of another's tower
But sometimes I am the tower you lean upon
I help you when your faith seems to have gone
I am ordinary Spirit walk with me every day
They are by my side come what may
Helping to overcome life's twists and turns

Allowing me to see, understand and learn

I am ordinary; I am a channel of light

Like you I work with Spirit day and night

The difference may be I have knowledge of this

And without it I would feel something was amiss

But you see a common mistake is often made here

And I would like to make it abundantly clear

Just because you don't sit, channel or hear your Guide

Doesn't mean Spirit aren't by your side

For we all work for Spirit, every single one of us

To be profoundly aware isn't a must

A smile passed onto someone low

Will help that person's life to flow

A word in the ear at the right time and place

Can put a smile on the most downturned face

Spreading love and the act of giving

Helps Spirit to reach out to the living

So you see no one has a special gift

We all have the ability to uplift

Anyone who professes that 'they' do the healing

Or has a superior attitude leaves me reeling

Quite simply lack understanding of this physical plane

For all messages, miracles and acts of healing to ease pain

Come directly from Spirit and Angels of light

These Guardians will never give up the fight

For I am ordinary just like you

I have nothing special, nothing new

I am ordinary; I am a channel of light

Like you I work with Spirit day and night

Journey

When I was small, I loved to live
My heart was wide open
I felt no different than you
There was never a need to hide

But as I grew I began to see
That people saw me differently
The stares, the comments, the watchful eyes
They all came as a huge surprise

I never asked to be like this
It's not my fault I cried
Mum and dad always held me close
But I was dying inside

At school the jokes came thick and fast
When teams were picked I was always last
Isolation became a familiar friend to me
I wanted to scream, just leave me be!!

I began to believe all the things that were said
Self-hate began to fill my head
So around myself I built a wall
And behind it I cowered, ever so small

Marriage was offered I took it fast
In my heart I knew it could never last
Someone to love, to hold me close
Little did I know this would damage me most

As the years flew by
Many times I asked myself . . . why?
I got lost in the darkness that had always been there
Not a soul I thought, did anyone care

Then a glimmer of light
Someone saw my plight
A hand to hold
They bought me in out from the cold

Slowly I began to see
That not everyone had hated me
Like a bird my wings began to unfold
And life began to hold riches untold

Slowly my wall
That over the years had been built so tall
Began to fall down
So now a smile I wear instead of a frown

Yes, I look different than anyone else
But now I refuse to be a mouse
The climb has been steep
And sometimes, still I weep

But now for the moral of this tale
I hope my message will not fail
Short or tall, fat or thin
We should *always* see the beauty within

Be my friend is all I ask
Then my feelings I won't have to mask
Please don't give me your pity or sorrow
Maybe then there will be a brighter tomorrow

So when you see someone with something amiss
Just promise me to do this
Say hello and offer a smile
For it will certainly make their day worth while

Forgiveness

There have been times in the past
When I had lost my faith in everything
I thought I wouldn't make the distance
Praying each day would be my last

The dark clouds that surrounded me
They were my only friends
Keeping out the sunshine
So that I simply couldn't see

I thought I wasn't worth it
To fat, to thin, to ugly
My world was cold and empty
A lonely bottomless pit

At least the bruises I could hide
In fact through choice I didn't mind
But mind games are so very cruel
Useless, worthless, silently I cried

I had a choice to make
Stay and be broken, go and be free
I will *not* be beaten
This life is mine, not yours to take

When I broke free, all hell broke loose
With my courage in both hands
I took my first steps all alone
Finally, I had escaped the noose

It has been many years since that day
And I have changed so very much
Now I *put* my faith in everything
My world is different in every way

I have moved on to pastures new
With hand on heart I do forgive
I am so much stronger now
The sun is out, the sky is blue

I am lucky I have found my way
My road is not always straight
Up and down and round the bends
But my faith, I know is here to stay

It's always easy to believe
The hurtful things that people say
Their spiteful words can cut so deep
A web of hatred they can weave

For those people I do ask
Take no notice, close your ears
Open your heart, try to forgive
With practice this becomes an easier task

Our light inside, it burns so bright
Together we must stand tall
Side by side, united with love
Can you imagine what a beautiful sight

Our purpose here is to learn
The lessons can be hard
We all have chosen which way to walk
And with each decision we make a new turn

The hardest thing in life to do
Is to love yourself
Be honest and open
Most importantly be true to you

Be kind and thoughtful every day
Have faith in who you are
Spread love and light to everyone
And together we can keep hatred at bay

My intention is not to make you feel sad
But to try and help you to understand
That we can send love and forgiveness
To all those people who make us feel bad

What Do You See?

As you stand and look at me
Tell me what do you see?
Do you see my happy face?
Maybe you see through the smile I have in place?

Can you read my eyes?
Do you hear my cries?
Would you feel my touch if I reach out?
I wonder, could you hear me if I shout?

Do you know how I stumble and fall?
Maybe you don't notice at all
Can you hear the words I speak?
Will you ever understand how I feel a freak?

Maybe sometimes I find it hard to cope
Surrounded by misery, deserted by hope
Everyday living a lie
Letting life just pass me by

All my life I have worn a mask
Taking it off will be no easy task
The shadows cast around me by my youth
They cloud judgement, hide the truth

I hate attention and all that it brings
I see me as you see me, it makes me cringe
But when I see people take centre stage
I so want to unlock the door, get out of my cage

Everybody says how easy it can be
But you don't understand, you're not **ME**
Every day I want to turn and run
My hands are tied, to my head is held a gun

I don't care what you say
I know that every single day
The same people, they point and laugh at me
I silently cry for I can't let you see

If I had one wish, just for myself
I wouldn't ask for money or good health
My wish would simply be
To look ordinary, not odd like me

I may look happy, I've had years of practice
But the truth is I am often an actress
Always scared and unsure
Wondering, today what unkindness I will have to endure

I am all alone in this place
I use my hands to cover my face
Crouching in the corner feeling small
You are deceived if you think I stand tall

So tell me . . .
As you stand and look at me
What do you *really* see?
Can you read the message in my eyes?
Can you hear my silent cries?

Alone

Why am I sitting here all alone?
Aimlessly my thoughts seem to roam
They take me to some strange places
Grabbing hands, unfamiliar faces

They all seem to want a piece of me
Everyone looking on with glee
Is there anyone on my side?
I am alone, I must run and hide

I go further, deep inside my mind
I'm now scared of what I might find
Deeper and deeper I have travelled
My innermost secrets being unravelled

I don't want to see what is unveiled
Seeing everywhere I have failed
Why are my thoughts so cruel?
This fire inside doesn't need any fuel

But on and on the punishment goes
Through my veins the poison flows
I try to put a shield around my heart
Too late it's been pierced with a poisoned dart

I can feel my heart wither and die
Yet I am still breathing, I wonder why
Maybe I am here to learn?
If so the indignation burns

I can taste my fear
There is no escape from here
I try to close my mind
Too terrified of what I might find

What are you trying to say to me?
Why are you ignoring my plea?
These horrible images from my past
Are they breaking free at last?

They are upon me now
I need to face the truth, but how?
I reach out my hand to you
You were always there, I didn't have a clue

I feel so relieved, you heard my call
You are like my shield, standing tall
Teaching me to believe in myself
Helping unlock my heart to untold wealth

One by one I shall face my fears
Knowing that you will wipe away my tears
Picking me up when I fall
Answering when I call

I now know that I am not alone
With you by side, never will I be on my own
The path ahead is long and steep
But with your help my strength I will keep

My love for you knows no bounds
You keep me calm as my heart pounds
Nothing from you can I ever hide
Thank you, my loving Spirit Guide

The Darkness

The darkness brings with it uncertainty and doubt
Shadows cast by the eerie light
You sit here alone in the depth of the night

Close your eyes and try to dream of what should be
But your unwilling thoughts lead you back here
A place where you are all aware of your fears

The fight that helped overcome the highest hurdle
Has deserted you; left you high and dry
Bitter tears of loneliness is all you cry

Opening unwilling eyes against the dark
What's that you see in the corner of your eye?
Gripped with fear your mouth goes dry

But in truth there is a part of you that wishes
That whatever you imagine lurks in the darkness
Claims you; takes away from this mess

You see the beauty of release
Something that will take away the unbearable pain
Too late now your thoughts are on a runaway train

Speeding towards an unknown location
Gathering pace with every passing day
Quietly you face acceptance; there is nothing more to say

You wonder where the person that you once were has gone
Maybe this is the real you; who you have been all along
How could everything now be so terribly wrong?

Feeling the familiar stab of jealousy
Why can't you be more like them?
They shine like a diamond, the most beautiful gem

You however; you are the mud from which the stone was extracted
Only useful for a short period of time
Then forgotten; unlike a diamond you don't shine

Turning your back upon the world is so much easier
Feeling yourself slipping; you have lost the will to hold on
Nothing inside left; empty all gone

The darkness brings with it uncertainty and doubt
Shadows that are cast in an eerie light
Sitting here alone in the depth of the night . . .

Think

When you get up and the sky is grey
And you are hurt by the things another has to say
Try to take heed from the lesson being taught
Sometimes things are said or done with little thought
And the consequences of a certain action are played out
Leaving you in very little doubt
That once again it seems you are left with a bitter taste
Sometimes we are all capable of doing something in haste
I am sure everyone can recall when they have caused pain
But only if we learn lessons can we gain
As a race our biggest fault is to not think of another
Turn our back when I goes wrong and dive for cover
Think about another with every deed
Are you motivated by selfishness or greed?
Could you take the time to stop and think?
Sometimes what you say or do could affect another close to the brink
I am as guilty as anyone here
I have said things out of anger or fear
I have done things that I regret every day
I know I could have done things in a different way
But I didn't and paid the price
The one thing it did was to make me think twice
I am now very aware of how another could react
To say something I may or do without tact
You never really know what has gone before
And as we never ever truly know the score
Would it be too much to ask to look before you leap?
If you do so I can guarantee the benefits you will reap
We are by nature driven by love and hate
If we all operate upon that love maybe happiness won't be such a long wait

If you are the person that feels hurt
Left feeling alone when words are curt
Try to see that something good could come out of this
Maybe another was due to learn a lesson at your expense
Maybe their journey needs to progress
They need to hurt themselves a little less
However much it causes pain
You will rise, face another day again
We have to keep moving forward to progress
Its just that sometimes we don't see what for us is best . . .

In every thought there is a rainbow

In every word there is truth

In every deed there is kindness

In every dream there is hope

For My Friend

As I sit here and think of the friendship we shared
And the countless ways you showed others you cared
A solitary tear runs down my cheek
I realize that all too often you felt small and weak
But in truth you were a giant
You never realized and was always the one who was compliant
I sat with you and held your hand as you cried
But through it all your faith in others never died
Always seeing the good never the bad
I wish with all my heart you could have seen the beauty you had
But the pain in your heart got too much for you to bear
This I understand even though it seems so unfair
Life for you was a struggle day after day
The light in your heart was never enough for you to find your way
I truly hope that the place you have now journeyed to
Has allowed you to see something that we all knew
And as I now look at the sky every night before I go to sleep
I will endeavor to smile for you instead of weep
For I know that wherever you are you will be smiling now
The permanent frown will have left your brow
So goodnight and God bless my beautiful friend
The light you have left behind will shine forever never to end . . .

Protector

I really hate feeling like this
My insides, they bubble and hiss
This hate that seems to consume me
It blinds, so that I cannot see

I have this ball inside my chest
Thumping and screaming, it won't let me rest
I desperately need to set it free
But I can't, it just won't let me be

There is a voice inside my head
It tells me to close my ears to what's been said
I try so hard, I really do
But I can't, so I simmer and stew

When they hurt the people I love the most
My former self become a ghost
I don't like the person I become
But I'm their protector . . . I'm their mum

I want to say some nasty things
To see the misery that it brings
To see the pain in their eyes
Then I will be deaf to their cries

But I know that way down deep inside
My heart will always be my guide
Never could I say those things
The alarm bell of my conscience rings

Why do people cause such pain?
Surely true friendship they will never gain
Playing people against each other
When we are all sister and brother

As I watch my children suffer
I try as hard as I can to be their buffer
But they have to learn
That true friendship you have to earn

As I stand and watch this unfold
I realize how people can be cruel and cold
Sometimes I wonder if my kids are way too sensitive
But no, I am proud they are loyal and know how to give

As parents we all need to see
That one day these saplings will become a tree
How they turn out is in our hands
Only their beauty should grace these lands

Feed them with values, trust and love
And they will be like the angels above
Feed them with selfishness, hate and greed
Then you will sow an ugly seed

Admiration

As I stand and watch
My admiration raises another notch
You always share your sunny smile
Yet I know life for you is a trial

Often you stop and look at me
I know that you know I see
All the pain that's hidden in your eyes
You know I don't believe the lies

Your loyalty is to be admired
The load is heavy, I know you get tired
The road for you is always uphill
Day after day you swallow a bitter pill

Never a chance to go out and play
Indoors doing the chores you have to stay
I wonder what you really feel inside
Always looking in from the other side

I see your spirit burning bright
You must stay strong and fight
The battle you wage is within your heart
When the time is right you will make a new start

Even though we don't say a word
All your troubles I have heard
Sometimes you look at me, feeling small
There is no need you have every reason to stand tall

Always allow your heart to be your guide
There will forever be people on your side
And every corner in life you turn
There will be a valuable lesson to learn

You are at the beginning of a long journey
A bright future you find hard to see
But I have seen it in your eyes
Follow your heart, for that is where the answer lies

Rain

I went for a walk today
Trying to cope with my inner pain
Feeling sorry for myself
Quite suddenly it began to rain

Brilliant, I thought
That's just my luck
My mind was going round and round
Like a record that has got stuck

Why ME again. I thought
As the sun is shining bright
Just as things are going well
My world has turned as black as night

My climb seemed very long and steep
I lifted my face and started to cry
It seemed to wash away all my troubles
The rain felt good, I thought with a sigh

That day I saw the world in a different light
If the rain helps nature while it is sleeping
Then the darkness and gloom is not what it seems
Had I found the answer I had been seeking?

It's nice to think that our life will be easy
But how will we ever learn
A long straight road, no troubles ahead
Never a new page to turn

Things will be sent to try us all
And the road may seem to be long and hard
But there is always a lesson to be learnt
Sometimes it is good to let down our guard

This beautiful land in which we live
Will surely die without the rain
It would be barren and empty
And we would have nothing to gain

We are like nature
We need to grow
The lessons we learn
Are the seeds that we sow

Next time that it starts to rain
Try not to see it as dark and bleak
Let it wash away your troubles
Maybe then you will find the answers you seek

Sometimes

Sometimes I wonder what would happen if I let my smile slip

Sometimes I wonder how it would feel if loneliness lost its grip

Sometimes I wonder what it feels like to be free

Sometimes I wonder how many people truly know me

Sometimes the I don't like myself at all

Sometimes I wish at my hurdles I would be allowed to fall

Sometimes I wonder if you ever see my tears when they fall

Sometimes I wonder if you actually really care at all

Sometimes I see the hate in your eyes and try to figure out what I have done

Sometimes I feel like I am looking down the barrel of a loaded gun

Sometimes I feel pity for you

Sometimes I think you really don't have a clue

Sometimes your actions take my breath away

Sometimes my eyes sting at the words you say

Sometimes my heart is filled with such sadness at your hate

Sometimes I wonder if it's just too late

Sometimes you will throw me some kindness

Sometimes even that is under duress

Sometimes I wonder where you have gone

Sometimes I tell myself it is me that is in the wrong

Sometimes I just wish with all my heart and soul

Sometimes all I want for once is to feel whole

Sometimes we all have to put ourselves out

Sometimes the best way forward is to listen not shout

Sometimes we have to consider how others feel

Sometimes life is about understanding others have a far worse deal

Sometimes my love I wonder if you are just too blind

Sometimes I think maybe I am just too gullible and kind

Sometimes for you and you alone I pray

Sometimes my greatest wish is that you keep your negativity for me at bay

Sometimes all the Angels are at your side

Sometimes even from them you hide

Sometimes just sometimes all I want is to see you smile

Because when you do it is like a rainbow and I love to rest there for a while . . .

Wealth

Every person that reads this verse
Is rich beyond their wildest dreams
Stop what you're doing, wherever you are
Do you really know what the word wealthy means?

Some people think that money
Can buy us everything
They are convinced by the happiness
That they think it will bring

There are many people
Who think that way
It doesn't make them bad
If only I had . . . they often say

Some people want for nothing
They have all that money can buy
Still they are not happy
I'm sure they wonder why

When we are born into this world
We have no material wealth
No clothes, no money
If we are lucky we will have good health

If we all could stay that way
And enjoy the beauty around us
To see the riches that we already have
Try to leave behind the noise and fuss

There would be no need
For anyone to compete
We would all have the same
Never any expectations to meet

There are all sorts of people
In the world we live
Money in our pocket or not
Inside we are all rich enough to give

Look at the possessions that you have
They are easily bought and easily sold
So my friends remember
'All that glitters is not gold

Ray of Light

It has been a difficult few days
I have found it almost impossible to see through the haze
My thoughts in constant turmoil
Memories I don't wish to spoil

But sitting here in the fading evening light
I still struggle with my inner fight
My mind is telling me to let go
But how I just don't know

Every time I try to switch off my mind
I can't, to common sense I am blind
Thinking so many times; 'what if?'
This dreary fog just won't lift

As I look up I see the clouds are gathering above my head
They are dark and gloomy, the colour of lead
Why is it I have this space within?
Why is personal happiness to me a sin?

Every time something starts to go well
I end up in my own personal hell
It all falls apart around my ears
Confirming every last one of my fears

It seems I can fix it for everyone else
I just can't gain control in my very own house
Don't misunderstand I do not moan or berate
I love to give a helping hand to fate

To help others along their pathway and find true love
Is wonderful and I thank the Angels above
That I am able to help others in this way
But just once I would like that love to with *me* stay

So I can have someone to hold me close
And share innermost thoughts of what I want most
Someone who will love me no matter what
Dressed in rags or riches they won't give a jot

Someone to accept me just the way I am
Does it really matter that I am not flashy or glam?
That sometimes I find it difficult to express myself as I could
That I need help to step away from my cloak and hood

There must be someone out there who could love me
Or I am I destined forever on my own to be?
Never sharing as my heart desires
Never feeling the flames of another's fire

Am I just day dreaming of what could be?
From this personal prison will I ever be free?
For it seems to me that I am a first class friend
And wonderful if you want a broken heart to mend

But anything else just passes me by
Since I was at school I have asked myself why
Rarely being the one to choose
The one I wanted I would always lose

For I obviously have not got what it takes
To compete in a world where they want to be no more than mates
I obviously fall way below the watermark
I paddle in the shallows, in the dark

As my thoughts take on a more pitiful tone
I realize I am not alone
My Guide has come so very close and is at my side
He is wearing a smile oh so wide

I ask why he seems to be laughing at my troubles
He just whispers something about bursting bubbles
I am confused, don't know what he means
What bearing have bubbles got upon my dreams?

He tells me in a calm and loving tone
That I have allowed my despondency to grow
And that I have placed myself inside a bubble
And there I hide my thoughts in a muddle

My way forward is to look back into my past
To understand why nothing has ever really seemed to last
Why I seem to be drawn to those who need a prop
And without help they would inevitably drop

To learn to be strong and put aside what I seem to want the most
He will always be there guiding never leaving his post
To maybe for a short while not concentrate upon 'forever'
But to have fun and never say never

For this could open my heart and mind in so many ways
It doesn't hurt to occasionally play
To live my life day to day with laughter
By doing this eventually it will lead to my happy ever after

I sit back and think upon his wise words
I have listened but have I heard?
I suppose in truth in forever searching
From situation to situation I have been lurching

I must now burst that bubble
Try to put behind me all the troubles
That have dogged me from my youth
Time to face the truth

One day I hope my dream will come true
But for now I will concentrate upon pastures new
Have some fun and live a happy life
Leave behind the negative thoughts that were running rife

For I have now gained a new Inner Sight
I have found my wonderful *Ray of Light*

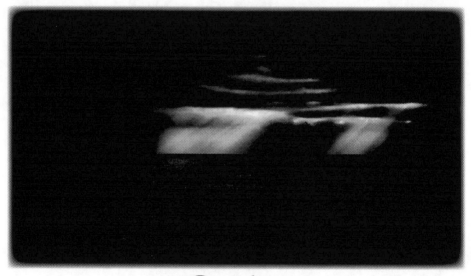

Ray of Light
©Shane Turnbull

The River

Sometimes deep, sometimes shallow
But constantly always flowing
Crystal clear or muddy depths
The seeds of life you are always sowing

Where are you going?
Will your journey ever end?
How long will it take?
What messages do you send?

Over the hills, into the woodland
Through the darkness and back into light
Always you keep going
Whether it is day or night

You hold such beauty
And such grace
We may look but do we see
The wonder of this place

Many things do you see
And the life that you give
Helps nature and animals
Giving everything a chance to live

People may build a dam
Still you find a way through
Over the top or underneath
Nothing will stop you

Without the blood in our veins
We would start to wither
Without you nature would die
For you are, The River

The River
©Shane Turnbull

Waterfall

My tears run like a waterfall
I try yet still I don't hear your call
I thought you were meant to be by my side
Why do you choose now to hide?

I need you to make sense of a situation gone bad
How can I possibly treat it as a passing fad?
When, unintentionally I invested way too much
And now it's too late, no going back I need your words so much

I sit here all alone listening intently
Wondering if you are guiding me gently
Hoping you are wrapping your hands around my heart
Trying to remember we are never truly apart

How could I have been so blind?
In truth I never really understood until I crossed the line
By then it was way too late
No point once the horse has bolted in closing the gate

Now everything lay in tatters at my feet
I wish I could rewind and not repeat
But I have to swallow the medicine you give
And accept the lesson, move on and live

So if I need to learn from my mistake
And yet again oh how difficult life you make
What can I do to heal myself?
I miss your words and their worldly wisdom and wealth

Stupidly stupid I know I am, in truth I heard you whisper in my ear
I ignored your warning that is abundantly clear
Maybe next time I shall listen more closely
Ignore what I want mostly

For the lessons you teach me every day
Get harder and harder this is an impossible game to play
I miss the boat every time
I don't mean to winge or whine

Maybe I should go and live in the mountains of Tibet
Is that how I need to pay this heavy debt?
Keep myself away from things that hurt
Live among mother nature, the trees and dirt

At last I hear you whisper a word or two
About moving on to pastures new
I am trying to head your advice
Always, always think twice

The situation will force me to take a step back
Watch from a distance is my defense, my attack
It saddens my heart but I know you are right
I need to keep reality in sight
Foolhardy gestures are misguided and will add to the pain
And in the long term nothing will be gained
My Spirit Guide I now hear your voice
And understand we all have choice

Good or bad we must stand tall
Never allow ourselves to fall
I will miss you my friend but it has to be this way
You understand what I am trying to say

I had little understanding before
As to what lay behind this particular door
Now I know and there is nothing to be done
I have to self-protect look after number one

I shall stand on the sidelines and watch with interest
But for now distance even when standing together is best
So this is my heart saying goodbye
I do it with a heavy sigh

Maybe in time our paths will cross once more
In fact of this I am sure
I trudge my lonely pathway ahead
Feeling better for what I have said . . .

Be Free

What will I do? Where will I go from here?
Do I just wait for someone to dry my tears?
Will the pain ever leave my wounded heart?
Will I ever be able to once again start?

The future doesn't seem incredibly bright
When I know that I have such an immense battle to fight
Do I keep my thoughts buried deep?
Or do I confess that I am finding the hill to steep?

My mind is a treacherous thing
Negative thoughts it brings
Again and again I try to find my way out
Not really sure what it's all about

I can't seem to pick myself back up
I need a change of luck
To turn myself around
Get my feet back on solid ground

But where do I look to first?
I can't stop fearing the worst
I need something that will help me to see
Something that enables me to set my mind free

I want, just for a minute to leave it all behind
To be free from the constraints of mankind
To wander through the wilderness
With no other problems that press

To breathe in the beautiful clean air
To be able to be without care
To find myself upon a cloud taking a ride
And just because I want to down a rainbow slide

To sing with the whistle of the wind
To still see when Mother Earth's lights are dimmed
To feel the water run through my fingers
Just to be able for a little while to linger

To be in a place where nothing is feared
And to have such love so abundant, so near
To know my actions are not judged
Where along my pathway I am gently nudged

To see the pattern of what has gone before
And to see what is yet to beseech our door
To be able to understand why
Some things have to happen to make us cry

So that we can truly understand
What for us has been planned
Is only what we need to experience to learn
And with each one strength and courage we will earn

Making our journey easier to bear
Each battle won we gain another feather in our hair
Another string to our bow is a good thing
And can only with it wisdom bring

I wished to be taken to another place
If only for a moment to touch base
But I realize that I can go there any time
And that tranquillity I will find

For it is just a whisper away
Always there, night and day
I can travel there as often as I please
Everything there for me to see

All I have to do is open my eyes
And see the eagle as it fly's
Allowing the wind to take it in the direction it blows
I am sure that where it will end up it doesn't know

But faith, the mighty bird does possess
Nothing more, nothing less
It will find its way whichever way the wind doth blow
The new direction sometimes needed in order to grow

My life right now seems to be troubled
And my fair share seems to have been doubled
But now I know I can visit my special place
And find the strength for my troubles to face

For the world in which we live
Has everything we need in order to give
Either to others who need a shoulder on which to lean
Or to ourselves to reach our goals, fulfil our dreams

The strengths I gain I have yet to find
The question of what to do still occupies my mind
I am sure it will in days to come
But I need to pick up the ball and with it run

To see where this latest journey will take my feet
And what challenges upon it I will meet
As long as I keep my head held high
And learn to let go when I need a good cry

My strength and love will help me find my way
My resolve, I am sure will win the day
When I reach the place I meant to be
I hope the lesson learned, I will see

My mission here is to pass on the lessons I learn
And to help others understand when it's their turn
That the life we live is filled with what we need
To enable us to spread the word, sow new seeds

Linked together to the Great Spirit making us one
All walking together under the same sun
Finding along the way love, peace and harmony
For, you, me, them and us, we are all indeed family

My vision of what one day will eventually be
Is that our spirit will be able to run free
Our ego will be a thing of the past
No longer over us a shadow to cast

Working together for the good of everyone here
No famine, greed, poverty, war, violence or fear
The beauty of our Mother Earth shall unfold
Then we will see the true riches she does hold

I have faith that my world is as it should be
Even though at the moment I can't see the wood for the trees
But the sun will eventually shine through
Unveiling truths that deep down I already knew

Applying the lessons is what I must do
To myself be honest and unreservedly true
Helping others to gain their sight
All joining together so our future is bright

My troubles are a drop in the ocean compared to some
But every single one I overcome
Will prepare me for my road ahead
Equip me for the path I am intended to tread

So join me in seeing our world as it should be
It will not be easy, this I agree
But **TOGETHER** we can live in the world I spoke of before
And like the eagle, to new heights we will soar

Link hands and hearts with everyone
Try to forgive, I know this isn't easily done
Reach out to those in need
Learn from man's lessons about hate and greed

One act of kindness that each of you sow
If passed on, can you imagine how that will grow?
One single candle can penetrate the night
Giving many who couldn't see the gift of sight

Picking someone up when they fall down
Throwing a lifebelt if someone is about to drown
All these acts have the potential to be passed on
By anyone, no matter whom you are or where you're from

Making our world a better place to live
The simple act of loving and learning how to give
My vision in this lifetime I may not see
But our children will pick up our legacy and hopefully one day
BE FREE

Children

I was given a message today
I think I understand what it did say
The following two children were using their voice
To express in different ways we all have a choice . . .

I dealt with a child today
Who seems to have lost his way
Screaming and shouting in my face
I heard someone shout 'he needs to learn his place'

Backed in a corner with nowhere to run
He screamed 'don' wanna' sit down, I wanna' have fun'
But in a short moment he caught my eye
I am sure he was silently asking me why?

Someone else tried to make him sit
That's when he lost it and kicked and hit
It was a pitiful sight to observe
The screaming finally hit a nerve

So many adults had entered the class
The screaming now so loud it could easily shatter glass
All these strange people giving him stick
I walked away slowly, feeling quite sick

I turned and observed the rest of the class
I don't know about them but I wanted to run, and fast
In the corner sat a girl covering her ears
She was sobbing gently; no one had noticed her tears

The screaming child was taken from the room
A stunned silence seemed to add to the gloom
A story was quickly pulled out and read
Everything forgotten as they concentrated upon what was being said

But still this little girl she did sob
I walked over to where she was sat
Taking her hand I gently lead her outside
We sat in the sun as I spoke I let spirit be my guide

That was very sad to see I softly said
Huge blue eyes locked with mine as she nodded her head
She took my hand and held it tight
As I looked at her I tried not to cry with all my might

Speaking quietly she said 'that little boy in there'
Is so sad and it seems no one cares
His crying and screaming makes me sad
Do you think the adults understand why he is mad?

Without another word she walked away
For a moment I was at a loss as to what to say
Then she came back with a flower in her hand
She dropped it softly and in the palm of my hand it did land

Smiling she said 'that flower is the colour of the sun'
I looked in her face and realised she knew her job was done
Together we went back inside
But now she wore a smile that was wide

She gave me a hug and skipped off to play
Once again I didn't know what to say
I wasn't sure who had helped who
But I have an inkling that *she* knew

At that moment in came the boy
Anger forgotten he was grasping a toy
He plopped down beside me vrooming happily
He pulled on my skirt 'come look and see'

As I crouched down to see what he had
He leaned forward just a tad
Placed his arms around my neck
Whilst giving me a hug, on my cheek he landed a peck

When it was time to leave for the day
They sat in a circle as normal to pray
The two children chalk and cheese
Were smiling and chattering with complete ease

One child so angry but minutes before
Was now sitting happily on the floor
The other, who had been distraught at his plight
Was listening and smiling with him, what a fabulous sight

I have re lived the situation again and again
Trying to understand the little boy's pain
And every time I see that little girl
With her crystal clear eyes and beautiful blonde curls

When I was weary and couldn't understand at all
I think that the she answered my call
An angel in disguise
She heard my soul as it cried

She didn't say many words to me
But what she said helped me to see
That she had reached out and felt his pain
And that by adults getting angry we have little to gain

We can stamp our feet and scream and shout
Underneath it all it's because we are filled with doubt
Or we can quietly shed a tear
Then gently let go of our fear

When someone directs their anger at you
Try to stay calm maybe they have pain to work through
If we swallow our frustration and sit tight
Then we can gently help them to see their light

From the children around us we have much to learn
That hostility often means that it is affection they yearn
By sending our love, compassion and faith to share
It will show that we really and truly care

Treat others as you wish to be treated

Hold out your hand to those in need

And you will sow a positive seed

Sitting By a Candle

Here I am sitting by a candle
With emotions I am finding hard to handle
Focusing my thoughts upon the flickering light
Asking for guidance to help my plight

The music in the background
Makes the most beautiful soothing sound
I let my wayward thoughts drift
Wondering if this fog will ever lift

My mind walks down a road it has been before
And stumbling slightly I walk through a familiar door
Behind it I find the most beautiful sight
The room is filled with gentle, soft glowing light

This room welcomes me with open arms
My body is alive I can feel the energy in my palms
From there it flows through my body and mind
Filling me up with thoughts of the positive kind

I open my eyes and before me an Angel stands
She is beckoning me forward, indicating we hold hands
I place my hands within her grasp
For a moment in the golden light I bask

A feeling of peace has flooded through me
I gently look up to her face to see
I can still hear the music it calms me so
And slowly, I begin to glow

Her smile has the warmth of a fire
I can feel myself float higher and higher
I look down at the room below
Smaller and smaller it grows

As I float onward feeling as light as a feather
I realise she is my shelter in my current stormy weather
Ahead I can see a light
As we draw closer I gasp at the beautiful sight

There before me lies a crystal bed
Towards it I allow myself to be led
Ever so slowly I sit down
Feeling the energy running through my toes to my crown

Every kind of stone must be here
From black obsidian to a quartz that's beautifully clear
Around my head an Amethyst pillow
As I look up I see a canopy of weeping willow

I close my eyes and drift away
No longer are my thoughts held at bay
Like opening a door in my mind
Letting go means I am no longer blind

I can see vivid visions before me
From them I am desperate to flee
But as I watch them slowly disappear
I realise that with them they take my fear

After a period of time I open my eyes
And standing before me to my surprise
Is a child, with beautiful golden hair
As I sit up am transfixed in a stare

Smiling she tells me that all will be well
She will always be there when I need to scream and yell
She tells me to let go of my negative feeling
And I will see more clearly with what I am dealing

Carrying on she says, this is the path you must tread
Even if the thought fills you with dread
But trust in me, when I tell you, you will not fall
You have the strength to scale even the highest wall

You know as well as I every new direction our life takes
Something new within us will eventually awake
Use these valuable lessons that you learn
Pass your knowledge on to others when it is their turn

It is now time to bid you farewell
In time this will be part of the story you tell
To help others when they think they will never cope
That they are never alone and to hold on to hope

I opened my eyes to see my candle still burning bright
Realizing that I now need to be strong and fight
I know that there will be always be bad days
When I won't be able to keep my feelings at bay

But somewhere in the back of my mind
I know that if I dig deep enough I will find
The strength to carry me through
If I am honest I think this I already knew

But if the knowledge I gain
Can help others when they feel pain
And it helps me and my family to grow
Then I am thankful for the seeds that have been sown

Time to BE

Why so sad little one?
What have you gone and done?
Has love deserted you once again?
Does your heart feel the pain?

When the night is at its height
I lie alone and beg to be shown the light
As the tears slide down my face
I plead for you to hear my case

Am I incapable of sharing my life?
As a mother, daughter, sister or wife?
My actions can be selfish and cruel
Sometimes it is with myself I have to duel

My heart is torn in two
I am lost and don't know what to do
Why do I turn upon those whom I love?
My hand sadly no longer fits this glove

I thought we had it all
It didn't take long for reality to call
Strip away the layers one by one
The ugliness is there, what have I done?

I can't run and hide anymore
I have to decide upon which door
I have to reach out and turn the handle
If I do will it extinguish this particular candle?

Deep down within my heart I know
Someone gets hurt whichever way I go
Will it be you or will it be me?
How much do I *really* wish to be free?

I don't want these feelings to turn to hate
At the moment I barely see you as a mate
We don't even talk anymore
My heart trails behind me on the floor

I can't look into your face
And see that special place
Did we really ever have it anyway?
Right from the start a game did I play?

I so don't want you to get hurt
But I see it in your eyes when my words are curt
I lash out at you and my words sting
I feel ashamed at the misery I bring

But you just will not see
There is much more . . . to me
I don't want to be in this place
You can no longer keep my pace

I want to climb to the top of the tree
To find what it's like to be free
But you hold on way to tight
It feels like you're restricting my flight

I love to feel the rain upon my face
To be free, see the beauty of open space
Your world is full of possessions, fixated upon wealth
Always determined to rob yourself of good health

You have no interest in what I do
So never do I bother you
You shut your ears to everything
Do you have any idea the misery that brings?

I sit on the side-lines and watch
My intolerance raises another notch
Where you are happy to let others do it all
I want to have a go, even if it means I fall

I thought this house would become *our* home
Aimlessly from room to room I roam
Nothing here seems to matter
My dreams in pieces, the mirror before me is shattered

I am feeling trapped, constantly going around in a circle
I gets me down I feel like a moaning Myrtle
Where is your fight?
Why just sit there as I stamp out your light?

My spark has returned
I am fed up with my fingers being burned
You never listen even if I shout
I am tired, all worn out

Should I stay, hanging on in vain?
Or do I move on, away from the pain?
Is it time to say goodbye?
Or should I give it one more try?

I am so sad behind this facade
Fed up with keeping this charade
In my heart I think I know it can't work
Behind my smile, my true feelings, they lurk

I want to run, be free from everything
To fix my heart so it can once again sing
Maybe it is time to start thinking about me
Placing one foot in front of the other maybe it is time to **BE**

Cry

You will never see the tears I cry
To you my eyes are forever dry
In my heart is where you will find my tears
Out of sight, silent to your ears

Many years ago I was told to cry was weak
I quickly learned to be silent and meek
Banish away any trace of feeling
This does not mean I don't give to you sincerest love and healing

I can see the pain in your eyes
I am not deaf to your heartfelt cries
My arms reach out though they touch you not
The tears falling in my heart are scalding hot

The road you now need to walk will be uphill
But a little hardship never did kill
If you keep going, get to the top
The view you find will make your heart stop

Upon your journey you must find the strengths you lack
Learn that when we take we have to give something back
Give freely with your heart and soul
And maybe next time you won't pay such a heavy toll

The sun will shine for you again sometime soon
Even if at the moment it feels as if your world is filled with gloom
These things are sent to try us all
It is up to us whether we stand or fall

My fight is now coming to an end
Now it's your turn to fight, no longer pretend
Stand up on your own two feet
Arise from your slumber you have challenges to meet

I will stand in the shadows, help pick you up if you fall
So long as you always remember to stand tall
We wouldn't know joy without pain
Wouldn't understand by being strong what we can gain

As we reach the fork in our road
It is time to set aside our heavy load
To walk separate pathways is how it has to be
Our hearts and minds need to be free

Free from all that has gone before
The woes and troubles that we placed at our very own door
Your journey of discovery is about to begin
I truly hope this is a battle you win

Never look back with regret
I will never be sad we met
One day you will see what I see before me
Someone who has such potential if you set your mind free

So go ahead and take your first step your future awaits
You have to keep your appointment with fate
New people you have to meet
Old demons to beat

My friend I will keep you in a corner of my heart
A little piece of us shall never part
We met when I was weak, now I'm strong
The journey has been difficult and long

So dry the tears from your eyes and take my hand
With every step forward the stronger you will stand
Don't ever think I don't care
Or that your sadness I don't share

For my love . . .
You will never see the tears I cry
To you my eyes are forever dry
In my heart is where you will find my tears
Out of sight, silent to your ears . . .

Dreams

Envy, how often do you have that thought?
You look at another and want what can't be bought
Or when they seem to have it all
It seems that you have nothing, feeling small

Anything is possible, whoever you may be
Do what you want and set your heart free
Allow your thoughts to be positive everyday
Fill your lives with colour, banish the grey

Try to open your mind to every opportunity
When you look you'll be surprised by what you see
The climb may be rocky and steep
But at the top your fortune you shall reap

Don't allow people to put you down
Always wear a smile, never a frown
You are special in every way
Don't ever forget that come what may

Always strive towards your dreams
Often things are not as impossible as they seem
Happiness is never measured in gold
But in our dreams that we hold

The Beautiful Dream

I had a beautiful dream
At my feet flowed a trickling stream
There were saplings either side
Behind a flower a small version of myself was trying to hide
As I followed the tiny stream I began to see
The tiny saplings were now young trees
And the stream, once trickling was now flowing
The other version of myself also growing
No longer hiding away
But in the shadows still I stayed
On and on I went the stream now gone
In its place a river wide and long
The trees now swaying gently in the breeze
Watching my other self more at ease
Up ahead I could see a glorious light
The sun had reached its midday height
Still walking onward I strained to see
I couldn't see the other me
But there up ahead I saw myself
No longer hiding, no more waiting upon the shelf
I was now running free
As tall as the now full grown trees
I stopped and stood back to take a look
A shiver of joy ran through me and I shook
Before me the river was now wider than ever and flowing free
Huge trees either side protecting 'me'
I could see straight up ahead, there was no bend
There didn't seem to be an end
Going on and on for ever and ever

True and strong whatever the weather
I awoke safely in my bed
A thousand thoughts whistling through my head
I decided the dream depicted my journey up until now and beyond
My link with Spirit an unbreakable bond
I could see far far ahead
And I knew this is where I was being led
So now I see myself as I was in that dream
As strange as it may seem
I was as tall as a giant tree
This is now how I wish to be
My journey started with me trying to hide
Now my friends, I walk in the sun, my smile is wide

The Beautiful Dream
©Shane Turnbull

My Best Friend

When I first saw you
My heart swelled with love
Surely, I thought
You were sent from above

Life will change for always
People kept saying
But I knew for certain
That forever you were staying

Yes, you've changed my life
In so many ways
The sunshine that you bring
Brightens every one of my days

You gave our family life
And our house became a home
We have all learned lessons
From the love that you have shown

You always listen, never judge
You comfort me through my tears
And completely understand
When I talk of my fears

Your gentle nature
Was given as a precious gift
And whoever you see
You always uplift

I look on with tears of laughter
As we wrap you in tinsel or dress you up
Never to bat an eyelid
You really are a laid back pup

Walking in the pouring rain
Barking at the cat next door
Digging holes in the garden
Muddy footprints on my nice clean floor

Jumping in mum's fish pond
I laughed until I cried
Watching you on the trampoline
I have a truly mad dog I sighed

But nothing would I ever change
You are my best and forever friend
We will be together always
Never will our journey end

As our Earthly mind does grieve

Hand on heart I do believe

That our loved ones are but a whisper away

Listening to every word we say

Wrapping their arms around us tightly

Brushing kisses on our foreheads lightly

Holding our hand as we silently cry

Willing us to understand their Spirit has not died

My Angel

For my daughter; Jordy . . .

I sit and watch you sleep
Your grace is there for me to see
I am fascinated by the secrets you keep

I sit and wonder why
Sometimes life for you is a trial
So hard to fit in, I want to cry

I sit and remember, it seems so long ago
How you used to laugh at the slightest thing
Now you seem to carry such anger and woe

I sit and wish with all my heart
That you find the direction you seek
When you find that path you can make a start

I sit and want to find every answer
The questions I have burn inside
However, you are the musician and I the dancer

I sit and feel that I am totally blessed
You have chosen me to teach
I hope that when the time comes I pass the test

I sit and wonder if anyone has eyes like yours
They see into your very soul
Do you realize, they make people stop and pause

I sit and watch as you smile
It is like being inside of a rainbow
I love to stop and rest there for a while

I sit and know what is true
You are an Angel, a messenger sent to teach
You carry in your heart colours of every hue

I sit and understand that as you grow
You will be part of a bigger plan
To share with people the knowledge you know

I sit and want to hold you close
For you are my child
And that is what I cherish most

For You, My Son . . .

The day you were placed in my arms
Was one of the happiest in my life
Your mop of black hair and big blue eyes
Your beautiful warmth, I even rejoiced at your cries

Every day discovering something new
Everyone seemed to have a different point of view
I had learn how to hold you in a different way
The nurses ever patient day after day

All manner of things were suggested to help
But eventually we found our way
Some people thought I would drop you
But I never did even as you grew

Our bond was instant
From the moment you arrived
In our crazy world which always seemed as black as night
You were my shining star providing a glimmer of light

Things changed as you grew
Our circumstances, our family, you were my glue
Your cheeky grin was always there
And when you slept, for hours I would stare

Knowing that if everything else was lost
We would have each other to call upon
I would dream about how your life would be
Determined that you would learn how to love and be free

From a baby to a toddler you progressed
I began to get concerned, you seemed different to the rest
You didn't seem to be able to talk
And I thought you would never ever walk!

Trying to get help was the hardest thing
Frustration upon frustration it would bring
With doctor after doctor I pleaded
Eventually I got the advice I needed

Many hours I used to sit and watch you
Wondering how you were going to get through
Seeing other children the same age
Reaching their milestones and onto a new stage

It was always harder for you
Nothing was easy, this I knew
But you would get there eventually
Very proud of yourself, showing off so I could see

School came upon us very fast
It seemed a long shadow around you was cast
Struggling to be able to fit in
Every race you seemed unable to win

Things got harder the older you became
All you wanted was to be the same
I could see the pain hidden in your eyes
And hear every one of your cries

I would cry all my tears for you
Even though you probably never knew
So sad that you felt so different from the rest
Even the smallest thing became a test

My fight for you was very hard
The system, it seems holds every card
But eventually after I had begged and pleaded
You got a little of the help you so desperately needed

The older you became it was easy to see
That your purity of spirit was always going to be
The most important thing in your life
Is to live in peace without trouble or strife

I know that I may seem to nag and nag
And that learning always seems to be a drag
But I am immensely proud of the person you've become
You walk to the beat of your own drum

If you had a choice, lose your personality
And from your problems be free
Then I would plead you to say no
I have watched you from a baby grow
And from day one when you were placed in my arms
I have been aware of your grace and charms
You always think of others first
Even if it means you come off worse
Don't ever be ashamed of who you are
You are a bright forever shining star

As you grow older you will see
What it truly means to be free
The sincerity and gentle nature of which you were blessed
Will carry you through your hardest test
But remember this most wherever you are
Be it close or from afar
I love you, and wouldn't change you in any way
And I will stand by your side night and day
Whether you choose to believe me or not
I wished for an Angel and that's what I got
I thank Spirit every day that to me you were sent
It has been more wonderful than I could ever have dreamt
So my son believe in all that you do
And all of your dreams I'm sure will come true.

The wheel of life keeps turning

When you have laboured up the steepest hill

The view at the top will take your breath away

Enabling you to face another day . . .

Nature

Take a look at the grass beneath your feet
It is beautiful and green
Hosting an endless variety of life
Only a tiny fraction of which we have ever seen

Trees that seem to stand the test of time
If they could talk what would they say?
The river that starts as a tiny stream
Is host to so much life day after day

The flowers that bend in the wind
And soak up the sun and the rain
They brighten up our world
As they flower again and again

Look towards the heavens and you will see
The birds so beautiful as they fly
And the clouds with a life of their own
As they skip across the sky

Everywhere we look there are animals to see
From tiny to enormous every one of them knows their place
If we don't care and look after our world
One by one they will disappear without trace

Each day take a moment or two
Look around you, what do you see?
Try to say a prayer of thanks to nature
For without it, where would we be?

Nature; **Wood Anemone**
©Shane Turnbull Photography

Nature; **Field Mouse**
©Shane Turnbull Photography

The Butterfly Fields

As I roam this glorious place
I see that this land before me
Holds so much beauty and grace

The birds so beautiful as they fly
I stand watching the clouds
As they race across the sky

Very often I come here to walk
If you listen carefully
You can hear nature talk

The message it gives is crystal clear
We need to live our lives with love
Not hatred and fear

Every animal, stone, blade of grass or tree
Live and work together, teaching us
That we too can live our lives in perfect harmony

Standing hand in hand
Together we should surely see
That we need to look after this beautiful land

Embrace the truth, forget the lies
We can then walk unhindered
In this, our paradise

Silently I listen as the angels gather round
Let us live our lives with love and light
Then maybe peace on earth can be found

Counting Blessings

One, two, three, four, five, six, seven
I could count all the steps to heaven
Upon every one of those steps lies a gift
Something I have been given to uplift
Maybe a lesson that was painful or sad
Or something that has made me feel bad
But a blessing it most certainly is
Enhancing my life, even if my actions, I have to quiz
Upon these steps I have found truth and love
Sent from Spirit and Angels from above
Some steps I have faltered upon and nearly fell
Others I have found such happiness I have had to jump up and yell
Everything we do, see, experience and feel
Has the ability to in some way help us move forward and heal
So my friends count your blessings every day
Up and up you will move on your own personal stairway
Will you ever get to the top?
Who knows, but why should that make you stop?
Blessings come in every shape and size
So look closely at what you are given and be wise
Turn a negative into a positive
Move forward you have a glorious life, full of adventure to live
Sometimes things are not exactly what they seem
Something that seems awful could eventually lead you to your dream
Blessings keep me going when I feel I have lost my fight
I know that eventually I will see the light
So climb up on high
Reach forward to grab your blessings and fly . . .

Spirit World

Toll the bell loud and clear
Everybody around must hear
The message I am about to give
Will help understanding of how we live

Once we have departed our physical form
It is as if we have been re-born
Back into our natural state
And for communication with you we wait

The world in which we walk
And the language that we talk
Is of utter peace and harmony
Our eyes are opened enabling us to see

We leave our ego behind when we return home
Our spirits are free to roam
There are no constraints here
We can be whom we are meant to be without fear

Children who return to us
Are well cared for; in this you can trust
They return to their earthly parents every day
And support and guide them in every way

The colours here are like nothing you have ever seen
Everything is beautiful; the air is fresh and clean
I will try and describe nature to you
But you will have to imagine your senses amplified by at least two

Take for example the humble flower
Have you ever really thought about its healing power?
Whether it be the most exotic and beautiful bloom
Or one of your weeds which seems to every one of your chemicals be immune

Its colour is a radiant thing
This alone is enough to make the heart sing
Often being drawn to the colour you need
And without realizing upon its energy you will feed

Standing in the sun absorbing the rays of light
Reaching up to its maximum height
Opening up petals that sing to your soul
Filling you up, making you feel whole

The grass is the most luminous green
And in it the most glorious insects preen
Little creatures you have never laid eyes on before
And every day even I discover more

The birds sing songs of love and peace
And send their vibrations in the hope pain will cease
They flutter their delicate and beautiful wings
And somewhere on earth someone's heart will sing

The animals that inhabit this place
Do so with the most Amazing Grace
The spirit in which they have returned
Remembering everything they have learned

They return to the Earth Plane day after day
As guides and helpers so others can find their way
Using their gentle spirits to guide
Unbeknown to most, standing by your side

The music; what a sweet and glorious sound
Filling you with riches abound
Lifting you up to the highest place
If you heard it, it would put a smile on your face

The water here is crystal clear
Our lakes and seas are made up of a million of tears
Not you understand ones that are shed in pain
Only tears of happiness, may I make that perfectly plain

The vibrations that the water here emits
Has the ability to instantly uplift
We sometimes bring it to you
To help in everything that you do

I could talk all day and night
About all the sounds and sights
I hope that you appreciate my need
To sow within you this visionary seed

But in reality it is not so far out of reach
Be in tune with your guides and they will teach
When you let yourself go into a meditive state
To look, listen and wait

One day before you, you will see
The birds, the water, the flower, even the bumble bee
They are but a heartbeat away
To see, open your mind, keep negativity at bay

Maybe in your dreams you will visit here
Speaking with others about your fears
Look around you very carefully
And maybe the fairies you will also see

Of course one day we all return to this realm
To discover who is truly at the helm
You will understand all that has gone before
And be eager to learn even more

But now the time has come
My channel is losing the beat of my drum
So I shall bid a gracious farewell
Glad that you listened when I tolled bell

I am . . .

I am with you when the night is long
I help you to see you **do** belong
I walk by your side night and day
I shine the light when you lose your way
I sit in the silence when you wish to be still
I hold your hand as you climb the steepest hill
I stand within your glorious light
I am your armour when you have to fight
I am your eyes when you cannot see
I hear you when you whisper your desperate pleas
I can help you lift any stone
I will ensure you are never ever truly alone
I will encourage you to walk through every new door
I will be your feather pillow if you fall to the floor
I am the voice inside your head
I will carry you if your legs feel like lead
I will help you find the words to say
I am still by your side even on the brightest day
I will be your blanket to keep you warm
I am your comfort when you are battered and torn
I will never tell you what to do
That my child is up to you
My job is to simply hold you close
And help you when you need it most
To give guidance and all of the above
But most importantly to shower you with love
To help you find your way
And on your true path stay
But never fear if you stumble and fall
Or if you feel you've hit a brick wall
Maybe that is the path you chose to seek

To help gain strengths when you were weak
There is a light that guides us all
It takes us places, helps us stand tall
Every living thing possesses this light
It burns inside whiter than white
Listen to your heart; find your true purpose here
You ears will open your vision will clear
I am beside you but a whisper away
Sharing your troubles and triumphs night and day
So close your eyes and drift off to sleep
For I am your guardian, all my promises I will keep
I am the one who stands with you in the sun
I am the one who has been with you since time has begun

Destiny

Do you believe in Destiny?
Or do you feel that *you* hold the key?
Do you think that some people are destined to meet?
Or maybe you and you alone are totally in the driving seat?

When you feel yourself inexplicably drawn to another
Do you accept it or run for cover?
Would you step forward, see where Destiny leads?
Or turn away, sure that such thoughts lead to foolhardy deeds?

Here is my, and only my view upon Destiny
I believe we are all meant to love and be free
All too often our hearts and hands are tied
Running around in circles pleasing others when they cry
There is nothing wrong in offering a helping hand
So long as it is not always you left alone to stand
Destiny will put people in your pathway to teach
Sometimes the lessons are hard to reach
And many years it will take until we grasp what needs to be learned
Then and only then a new page can be turned
Walking away from the people you have shared your life with can be hard
And I am sure in some way you will be left with a scar
But these wounds, they heal with time
Stepping forward takes courage and is no crime
Destiny I believe has it all under control
Even when the road is impossibly steep, emotions taking their toll
For around the corner a new doorway is ajar
This could lead you oh so very far
Even if it takes courage to walk through that door
You will forever wonder if you don't if it would lead to more
Destiny has thrown many troubles in my pathway thus far

But even through the pain and tears I still wait for my wishing star
For I believe when it arrives my lessons will have stood me in good stead
Helped me have a wise and true head
I am placed in others' lives as well as they in mine
And when the time comes they will say goodbye, cut the ties that bind
My destiny is still working toward its final destination
Until it reaches that place I shall walk this pathway with fascination
Looking, learning, loving and laughing, keeping my belief alive
That all will be well so long as I understand Destiny is unfolding as it should;
    I will survive . . .

Children of Light

A rare thing happened today
Something warmed me like the sun's rays
I read a book that truly touched my heart
The wise words written on the pages hit me like a dart
Something that lay dormant inside
Has now awakened, can no longer hide
There was a message that kept touching me
And if we lived our lives this way we could all be free
Free of every limitation that life brings
We could fly freely upon golden wings
Our lives would be so simple, everything clear
No one would live their life in misery or fear
This book was about children of light
They are arriving with amazing sight
These children are reaching out with their mind
Removing our blinkers, so we are no longer blind
They come back here time and time again
Helping us understand the potential riches we have to gain
Showing us little by little the power we posses
And how on our Spiritual pathway we can progress
These children unfortunately are hunted down
Having to leave their homes and towns
For man has discovered their many gifts
And want to use them for their own greedy benefits
But these children are not here to teach party tricks
Or to be used as a weapon in politics
They are here to bring forward a new way of living
Which primarily involves acts of selfless love and giving
Showing us the power of the mind
And how it can benefit mankind
If only more people could understand these souls of old

Learn from them; allow their true pathway to unfold
But I must have patience and understand
That all is happening as it has been planned
And that these children will slowly in numbers grow
Teaching some trusted souls all they know
Then eventually more will hear of these children of old
And across the world their story can be told
Then the roots of this beautiful love will spread
And paths of true enlightenment we will tread

The Rainbow Bridge

There is a place of which I have heard
Where every pet, from a bear to a bird
They run and frolic in the sun
Together they play, having endless fun

The fields they run in are lush and green
A place of such beauty we can only dream
There are dogs, cats and rabbits all here
Every animal to someone was once held dear

These are our beloved friends whom have passed away
They are no longer here to brighten our day
All ills and trauma have vanished without trace
They are full of spirit, love and grace

Every once in a while one will stop and stare
Listening to see who is there
In the distance is the person they have been longing to see
Their hearts are filled with glee

They turn their heads, eyes shining with happiness
Their joy and love, they have no trouble to express
They make their way over to where the lone figure stands
Who is waiting, holding out both hands

They meet again these friends of old
The reunion is a joy to behold
Reunited forever
Together, to be parted never

This is where we will once again meet
Our faithful friends we will warmly greet
For this is the Rainbow Bridge
Try not to shed a tear; you see your friends are always near.

Drums

The drums, they are calling me
Can you hear their steady beat?
Opening my mind, setting it free

They are taking me to another place
Never will I need to wear my mask
For here I am proud to unveil my true face

I can feel my body swaying
Coming alive with every beat
Connecting with spirit, healing, praying

The eagle as it glides across the moonlit sky
I am still for a moment in time
Surrendering to its presence as it passes me by

The fire is hypnotising, burning bright
I can feel its power inside of me
Enhancing my inner guiding light

The drums, they are part of me
As I dance around the fire
I feel alive, energized and free

Somewhere in the distance I hear a wolf cry
He walks with me every day
His strength, honour and truth, I know will never die

I can feel the dirt beneath my feet
Mother Earth dances with me
She is part of me; I can feel her heart beat

People from another time before me stand
They greet me as an old friend
And welcome me to their ancient land

A flute begins to play
The music is haunting, beautiful
The sun rises, the dawn of a new day

I am truly at peace
This music lifts my vibration
To a place where pain and hurt cease

We are honouring these bountiful lands
Together we are in perfect harmony
Never touching, yet forever holding hands

The drums are now beating to a new tune
I feel in touch with my very soul
As the sun rises we bid farewell to the moon

Time to go back, time to rest
I know that when I feel the need
I can go back anytime as their guest

I know my friends are with me each day
I feel their drum beats in my heart
They help me open my eyes, find my way

Angel Embrace

Have you ever sensed you were in an Angel embrace?
Were you aware of their soft feathers touching your face?
Did you feel the serenity they passed to your soul?
Helping you see it is possible to reach your goals

Maybe an Angel came to visit in disguise
Departing words of wisdom that were learned and wise
You possibly only met them for a moment or two
But what they said made perfect sense to you

What about the man who stopped to help when trouble called?
It doesn't matter what he looked like, fat, thin, hairy or bald
He could have been an Angel sent to help out
He heard you when you started to scream and shout

It could be that you see an Angel every day
Talk and communicate, listening to what they have to say
Encouraging you forward with quiet contemplation
Helping to resolve difficult situations

Do you see them in their heavenly guise?
Wings stretched out, magnificent in size
A gown of glorious colours they wear
A crown of golden light hovering above their hair

Could it be that you think Angels pass you by?
Never visit when you cry?
I can assure that this is not so
Whether you are feeling high, on top of the world, or incredibly low

They are but a whisper away
Ready to help night and day
Every person that graces this glorious land
Has their very own Guardian Angel on hand

All you have to do to is let them hear your voice
Out loud, or through thought, it's your choice
They will be by your side in a heartbeat
With open arms they will lovingly greet

I don't ask that my Angel lives my life
But hears me when dark thoughts run rife
I know that he is there by my side
And even if I don't physically hear, I know his wise words guide

He is also there to share my smiles
My triumphs, my happiness, the climbing of my stiles
I have met many Angels throughout my days
Flooding my soul with warmth akin to the sun's rays

This poem is to pay homage to that Angel embrace
It is indeed the most wonderful place
To let your soul drink in such love
Knowing its purity is directly from above

So if a feather floats down and lands at your feet
Then acknowledge that your Angel is waiting to meet
They are letting you know they are by your side
Supporting, lovingly helping to guide

Angels come in many forms please remember that
Not only people maybe a dog or a cat
Give thanks and acknowledgement you know they are there
And you will feel better knowing that someone *does* care

Special Place

Do you see the birds in the trees?
The butterflies; the bumble bees?
Can you see the grass that's green?
A more beautiful place have you ever been?

Can you feel a slight breeze upon your face?
We're moving too fast so let's slow our pace
There are a few clouds in the sky today
If they could talk, I wonder what they'd say?

Come with me into a world of light
Open your heart to this beautiful sight
Let go of all your troubles
Allow them to float away in big shiny bubbles

Let the sound of silence ring in our ears
Helping us dispel our fears
Let the love of life fill our souls
Helping us to fulfil our roles

Now take my hand
And together we shall explore this land
There is no rush, take your time
You are quite safe with your hand in mine

Open your wings and we shall soar up into the sky
Higher and higher we will fly
Look down at the land below
Smaller and smaller it seems to grow

Now we have reached that special place
This your own unique space
There's no need to fear, you've been here before
If you seek you can find the key to any door

Now I shall leave and be back in a while
Greet whoever you see with your beautiful smile
Sit in silence or invite them to talk
Or you could choose to go for a walk

Now it's time to be on our way
The light is fading it is nearing the end of the day
So say thank you to your host
They will always be there, never leaving their post . . .

. . . Now we are back safe and sound
Open your eyes and look around
Everything is different but still the same
When we open our hearts, we can only gain

Next time that you seek a quiet place
And you need your special space
Just open your heart
For you and your guide will never be apart

Healing

As I lay my hands on your heart
Let the glorious healing process start
All these beautiful rays of light
Filling your soul, what a wonderful sight

Calm yourself, feel the peace
Let those unwanted feelings cease
Take yourself to a world of dreams
Where nothing is ever what it seems

Let go of your troubles, cares and woes
Feel the energy from your fingers to your toes
Allow your thoughts to roam free
Never be afraid by what you might see

Sometimes you may travel to a faraway place
Where you will see a familiar face
Listen to the words of wisdom they speak
I am sure they have the answer that you seek

Maybe you will feel total contentment
Believe that these feelings are heaven sent
Angels will silently gather round
You won't hear a whisper, not a sound

Can you see that beautiful sight?
That is your soul burning bright
Remember that loving feeling
For I shall always be here whenever you need healing

Going Home

You came and our hearts you did touch
And you are missed so very much
Your smile, like the sun shall forever shine
And we know our hearts will heal in time

The kindness and love that you shared
Let us know how much you cared
And the memories that we have to hold
Will be held on to so that your story can be told

Our skies, they seem so very grey
And we wish that you could with us stay
But we know you will grace the skies above
Sending down showers of love

When our tears are falling
And with our hearts we are calling
Our only hope is that you are near
And that our thoughts and prayers you will hear

They say that angels are only on loan
And sooner or later they have to go home
So until we meet again, we shall say goodnight
Knowing that that your star will forever shine bright

Touching the Earth

There are many spirit children
Guiding the lives of others
Placing their hands upon their hearts
Helping to heal the pain of their mothers

It is a difficult concept for us to fully grasp
Why as spirit we should make choice
To be conceived, then never touch the Earth
Leaving parents bereft, never hearing their children's voice

Or only to be here for a short time
Then leave and find our way home
Leaving a wake of unbearable sadness
People feeling unable to cope; all alone

We are told that life is full of lessons
And from each experience we need to learn
Can such misery and heartache
In the long run really be doing us a good turn?

We may turn our head up to the heavens
Asking; what has anyone to gain?
Why us? Why me?
Surely it is punishment to feel this much pain?

But we are not aware that in our emotional state
Spirit does hear our call
They are always there, holding us up
Encouraging us to get up when we fall

Even if we lose our faith
Believing there is nothing there
.... we have been made to suffer
So why should we care?

They will be standing strong
Trying to help us to listen and open our heart
Moving us forward step by step
Encouraging us to reach for that new start

Time will pass us by
Old wounds will slowly start to heal
The pain will always be there
Little things reminding us how we really feel

Some of us will forever be in darkness
Never to find our way back
That could be the lesson we need to learn
To find and build upon the strengths we lack

Others will fight their way forward
Determined life will go on
Trying hard to understand, remembering before
That in their world there *were* reasons the sun shone

These children that leave us
When they are so tiny and small
They are in truth still here
By our side, always answering our call

Our very own Guardian Angels
Standing proudly in the light
The power of their love is so profound
Their soul, so pure, burning bright

Reaching out to give a helping hand
Wrapping arms around us when we're sad
You see, they never ever leave us
As on Earth—you will forever be; Mum and Dad . . .

Make You Think . . .

Isn't it funny how sometimes things make you think?
Something simple can redirect your thoughts
When you are teetering on the brink

The simplest of things can cause you to react
In a different way than you had intended
Stop you thinking about maybes and look at fact

We all have our burdens to bear
And feeling hard done by and angry
We will tell ourselves over and over life's not fair

We are sure that no one feels our pain
How can they? Our thoughts are a tangled mess
The dark clouds gathering and soon it will rain

But when we see how bad it *could* be
How others cope with such unbearable sadness
Don't you wonder how often they wish to be free?

I am sure they look around and wish that they could
Be just like you and me, only life's small problems to face
If circumstances permitted them to walk away, I wonder if they would

But often when things are really bad
The options are few and far between
And they have very little time for feeling sad

Getting up every day to face the same again and again
Putting on a brave face to the outside world
Standing tall and laughing loudly to hide the pain

Very few people will ever see their tears
For often they cry silently all alone
Scared others may turn their back when they talk of their fears

Marching on bravely day after day
Begging, pleading for a chink of light
They ask for a miracle when they pray

The most amazing thing of all
Is that these, beautiful brave souls
Will get up every single time they fall

We may look on with wonder at how they cope
But often instead of dreary desperation
They fill their lives with hope

I don't wish to imply that your climb is not steep
Or that the problems you have simply do not count
For I understand that often the direction our lives take causes us to weep

But sometimes when we don't know which way to turn
A wake up call is sent for us to see
And if we look and listen then from this we will all learn

There will always be someone who suffers more pain
This is what should help us to realize how lucky we are
And if we put our problems into perspective we will have much to gain

So next time you see or hear something that brings a tear to your eye
Remember that whoever you are hope burns eternal
And there will always be someone to hear your cry

There are no winners or losers in life

We are all loved, all guided

All part of the Great Spirit that guides our lives

Tick Tock

Tick Tock time is passing
Faster and faster it seems to go
Our lives are flashing by in a blur
What has happened to the ebb and flow?

Our lives seem to be filled with things
That often really quite insignificant
Wondering who said what to who
But not listening to any messages that have been spiritually sent

Not enough think about our Mother Earth
The world around us in which we live
A concrete jungle this place has become
Materialism makes it harder for us to give

Buildings and roads serve their purpose here
But unfortunately things have got out of hand
Of course we need shelter and transport
But we have blighted, too much our glorious land

It is all too easy to get caught up and forget
Life can easily get in the way,
Before you know it you're locked into a world of possession and greed
No longer hearing what Spirit are trying to say

Try to make sure you can get away from it all
Go and walk among the flowers and trees
Land your footsteps upon the grassy hills
Puddle your feet in crystal clear streams

Connect with the earth the way it was intended
Feel her as she breathes in and out
Let the peace of her enter your very soul
Allow the wind to gently blow away any doubt

If you do this you will find peace within yourself
A place that exists inside us all
It waits patiently, often for a lifetime
Intently listening for you to call

While in this sacred space take time to think
About who you are, what you do, who you want to be
Where are you going? Where have you been?
Is there anything you can change that will enable us to see?

Continue the journey discovering your deepest hiding place
It is here you will find all you need to know
The answers to your questions you will find
Enabling your true self to emerge and grow

When you return to your more materialistic life
You will do so with knowledge of your inner light
Will you take more time to stop and think?
Will you begin to see the colour in life not just the black and white?

Take time in your busy schedule
To get to know yourself in this way
And you can start to de clutter your life
Then you will hear more clearly what Spirit have to say

Understand that our Mother the Earth
Will always sustain us in our materialistic needs
If we treat her with love and respect
Listen to the warnings we need to take heed

Abuse her and she will wither and die
Love and respect her, she will open our hearts and minds
Allowing us to see the beauty in all that is here
Working as one, peace within as well as on Earth we can find

I See

I see the mountain before me

I see the river as it flows free

I see the flower opening up to the sun

I see the land that has been since time has begun

I see the Tiger by my side

I see the land change with time and tide

I see the beetle as he forages around

I see everything before me, riches abound

I see the clouds darkening for rain

I see the sun, a beautiful burning flame

I see the grass damp beneath my feet

I see everything from here, my seat

I see you as you rush from A to B

I only have to open my eyes to see

I see the cars and other vehicles you drive

I see your cities and some cultures thrive

I see hardship and starvation

I see many differences in every nation

I see despair and cruelty and weep

I see wounds to Our Mother that run deep

I see love and kindness that makes my heart glow

I see that some carry the knowledge I know

I see one person stand alone and strive for peace and harmony

I see the struggle for justice and to be free

I see the Tyrant who holds many under his boot

I see the frightened child with gun, forced to shoot

I see the struggle of the children in this land

I see the many who hold out a helping hand

I see what has become of Our Mother Earth

I see some with little or no self-worth

I see that there is always hope

I see that come what may, you will always cope
I see the love that needs to be shared
I see some filled with fear, running scared
I see the change that is upon you
I see the healing to be done on mass by the few
I see the world becoming a better place
I see things changing pace
I see you all living in harmony as one
I see the end of living by a loaded gun
I see the beauty that lies inside you all
I see many of you hearing Our Mother as she calls

The Tree

Step back and take a look
Are you a mighty oak standing tall?
Or the tiniest sapling
Extremely strong, but ever so small?

Our purpose here is the same
To touch the lives of others
To help and support our friends
For we are all family, sister, father, mother, brother

First there is the foundation
The ground beneath our feet
Feeding from the core of Mother Earth
Feeling the very vibration of her heart beat

Then we have the root
Without this we would die
Nurturing within us
Giving us the wings to fly

From the root we have our trunk
Growing stronger year on year
Supporting our foundation
Reaching upwards toward the skies so clear

Then we have our branches
So many reaching every way
Touching other peoples' lives
Each and every day

Upon each branch we have a leaf
That flutters in the breeze
Absorbing all the sunlight
Sending out healing energy with ease

Our lives are like the weather
Moving in cycles, sun, wind and rain
And like a tree we absorb it all
Even when lightning strikes we bravely take the pain

One tree standing all alone
May be more vulnerable than most
But many trees make a forest
Forming a united front, rarely leaving their post

Standing strong together
Branches reaching out
Sharing food and water
Showing each other what life is all about

The tree can be our salvation
When hard times come to call
Sitting at its craggy base
Or using the branches to break our fall

Like a tree if treated with love
We will grow strong and true
Standing solid, branches touching
Even if the strongest winds blew

But mistreat the tree
And it will wither and die
Leaving a blot on the landscape
Causing our Mother Earth to cry

Together we can make sure
That the saplings are natured with care
Growing together in our world family
In the knowledge that its *true* love that we all share

Connected by our spirits
That burn brightly day and night
Linking hands together
Ensuring our future is bright

The Tree of life; *Isolated Tree*
©Shane Turnbull

Saying Goodbye

Saying goodbye can sometimes be
The hardest thing to say
The words we need to speak
Can be difficult, our emotions get in the way

Whether we are saying goodbye
To a friend who is moving on
Or to a relationship that has run its course
We will feel empty when they have gone

When we lose someone to spirit
The pain can almost be too much to bear
Whatever the reason we are saying goodbye
Nothing will ever take that away the memories that we shared

Every person will enter our lives for a reason
What it is we often will never know
It could just be a few words that they have said
Or a lifetime of lessons that help us to grow

We will feel sad when they have departed
Maybe no one will ever take their place
You can rest assured as we move on
Inside us there won't be such an empty space

It can be difficult to see
That saying goodbye can be a positive thing
Standing alone we have to do it by ourselves
We gain confidence and new opportunities this can bring

Sometimes we are the ones to move on
Something leads us to pastures new
As we turn to say goodbye
We get to see it from a different point of view

Whatever the situation you're in
Whoever is saying goodbye
Try not to be sad, because as one door closes
Another opens, for what lies ahead we don't have a clue

Dry your tears and take a deep breath
Tomorrow is another day
Full of new dreams and people to meet
And words of wisdom to say

People will always come and go
But your memories you will hold on to
They may make you smile or shed a tear
But they will forever be true to you

But be sure that whoever you are
Whatever you do and whomever you have met
Saying goodbye is like saying hello
We should live our lives looking forward, and never with regret

The Good as Well as the Bad

Life is about taking the good as well as the bad
Accepting that others at some point will make us feel sad
But it is how we handle the situation at hand
And how stronger a stance was stand

This will determine how things will turn out
We need to wipe away any doubt
Have the courage to walk where others may not
Remember it is you not them who have to be happy with your lot

Sometimes I sit and dream about what may have been
The different things that I might have done and seen
If I had taken another route on my road
I wonder would I be carrying such a heavy load.

The answer to this of course I shall never know
But the road that I did choose has allowed me to grow
Sometimes I have not wanted to go on
My will to live seemed to have gone

But always I have come out the other end
My broken heart I realize I can mend
Picking myself up off the floor
Usually means opening a brand new door

Tentatively putting one foot in front of the other
Like a child looking for guidance from its mother
But when my confidence does return
I usually understand the lesson I needed to learn

Sometimes our destiny is not what we desire
And if we saw it all mapped out before us it would look dire
The hardest road can sometimes be the one we need
As it is surprising where it will lead

We do have choices of that I am sure
You can stand up and be counted or stay curled up on the floor
Whatever we choose is neither right nor wrong
We have to live our lives to our own song

It is never our place to in judgement sit
Or look down upon others, not one little bit
We have never walked in their shoes
Sometimes to their private lives people give away no clues

That person could be a tortured soul
Been thrown around like a rag doll
Even if they seem to have it all
Maybe, just maybe no one has ever heard their call

You see some people are put on our pathway
To help us find the right things to say
Or to teach us that not everything is black and white
And that our thoughts and feelings are not always right

I am no different than anyone else
I live an average life; have a family and a house
I expect no special treatment from anyone here
My life as yours is not always easy, my options not always clear

I have made the mistake in the past
To make decisions I knew would never last
But never has anyone ever helped by saying 'I told you so'
And muttering that 'you should have listened to me you know'

The people who have helped pick me up off the floor
Are the very same ones who encourage me to open a new door
Never do they berate me or shake their head
Or get stroppy if I ask for advice then appear to not listen to what's been said

They love me for who I am come rain or shine
And respect that the end decision has to be mine
They don't pretend to know it all
They just help prop me up when I am about to fall

So when you think to yourself 'that person is mad'
Or that you know the situation they are walking into is bad
Try not to bend them to your will
Sometimes we have to let others swallow a bitter pill

Just let them know that you will always be near
And that you will not sit in judgement, make that abundantly clear
You will help more than you ever know
By sowing the seeds of kindness wherever you go

Weakness

Whilst listening to music today
I had the most overwhelming feeling
That to feel weak as opposed to strong
Is sometimes actually ok

As a race we seem to imagine
That we have to always show a brave face
To say that everything is alright
Plodding on, facing situations we feel we will never win

There are times however in order to grow
We have to hold up our hands and admit
That the situation is just too much
And how to cope, we just don't know

There are the times when we feel weak
At our most vulnerable some might say
When we really want to shut out the world
Is when others advice or help we should seek

Our world is sometimes a strange place
As your moment of anguish, pain or sadness
Could be the opening to a new pathway ahead
And the help you seek may come from a new face

Have you ever thought the help you find
Whether it be from a friend old or new
Could be the direction they need to feel strong again
By helping you they will have a stronger frame of mind

How will we ever learn to receive?
If we never open our hearts
To gratefully accept what is being offered
Let go of our worries, learning how to grieve

How will we ever know the joy of giving?
If we never open our hearts to do so
Or extend the hand of friendship
To those who feel all is lost, life is not worth living

Once we have mastered how to give and receive
That there is room in our lives for both
That we don't always have to be a tower of strength
It will open up our mind and soul allowing old inhibitions to leave

Walking a new pathway ahead, knowing new trials will be faced
With the knowledge and understanding
That when we need help in whatever form
We will gratefully accept it when in front of us it is placed

This is the reality of recognising our strengths
That they often lie within facing our weakness
Understanding that sometimes we need others to give
And that to find happiness we don't have to go to extraordinary lengths

What Would You Do?

What would you do if you saw someone feeling low?
Walk away in a hurry or make the effort to say hello?
A few words of kindness may mean the world to them
You could make them feel so much better you know

Lending a helping hand to ease their pain
Making them understand that others *do* care
Showing them that there is hope
And that life doesn't have to always be the same

The feelings that isolation can bring
Can make even the strongest person fall
The loneliness can become unbearable
The silence in their lives making their ears ring

Looking back upon times gone by
Seemingly at one time to have it all
Wondering where it's all gone wrong
The same word repeating itself again and again . . . why?

Head held in hands silently the tears fall
Looking at themselves in a different light
Trying to take stock of their lives
Now heartache not happiness seems to rule

The path that they do tread
Always seems to be uphill
Putting one foot in front of the other is hard
Footsteps are heavy with legs feeling like lead

Just when it seems that life can't go on
Along comes someone to help them up
Building the bridges that they need
Afraid that if they blink they will be gone

Do they reach out and accept the helping hand?
Or do they reluctantly turn their back
Fear overwhelming them, afraid to ever trust again
Not believing anything could ever be different in their barren land

But if that help is persistent and will not walk away
Then hopefully at some point they will see
That often people do care and will go the extra mile
And they are willing to hear what they have to say

Sometimes they will only stay for a short while
Others they will go the distance
But trust in this, they will hold you up
And help to replace that frown with a smile

It's strange how things can change so fast
Dwelling upon what has gone by will only cause more pain
Returning to that place again and again
So whether the memories be good or bad, try to leave them in the past

But with courage and that helping hand
Their steps will become less faltering
The clouds will be white instead of black
And with more conviction they will stand

When the time is right and strength returns
Those thoughts and feelings can be explored
Taking each one out one by one
It may be hard often making their stomach churn

But if facing their own reality is what they have to do
Then help is always at hand
Guiding, helping, loving them at every turn
Helping to change their point of view

Their road will not always be easy, gliding along
There will be times when they feel all is lost
Back on their knees, once again crying out in pain
Asking where it has all gone wrong

If you are that person, try to put your problems to one side
Just for a short moment in time
And remember who you really are
You are a beautiful person with no need to hide

Think back to those people who helped you along the way
They never gave up, forever by your side
Even though you may not see them standing there
The support they gave helped turn your night into day

In those quiet moments try to rekindle your fire
This is just a blip, another bridge to cross
On the other side your rainbow awaits
Many hopes and dreams to inspire

The strength that we have inside us all
Makes it possible to walk a steady pace through life
Some will find it harder than others to stay on their feet
That is why we should offer a helping hand when we hear someone call

Friends

Some friends, they come and go
Sharing with us seeds of knowledge to sow
A brief moment in time when our paths do meet
A steady hand to help us stand on two feet

Friends that stick around through thick and thin
Laughing, crying, whatever the situation you're in
Always there, ready to catch you when you fall
Forever beside you, standing tall

Friends to share our joy as well as pain
They will dance with us in the sunshine and the rain
A true friend will love the good and bad
Our faults they will live with even when we make them mad

Don't take for granted your family
Without their support where would we be?
Brother, sister, father, mother these are you friends too
Come rain or shine they will always love you

Friends can come in any shape or size
Sometimes they are angels in disguise
A beloved dog or cat, to your heart they hold the key
They love you unconditionally, without them you would never be

We should count our blessings every day
For sometimes without our friends we'd lose our way
They can be a lone beacon of light
On a very dark and cloudy night

Remember that you are a friend to someone too
As friendship is a two way street, forever true
You are valued in a very special way
Each and every single day

Address the Balance

In life there is darkness and light
Blindness and sight
Happiness and sorrow
Yesterday and tomorrow

There are times when our walk is steep
And instead of smiling we weep
When the world seems desolate and cold
And we feel we have been rejected from the fold

The world can feel a lonely place
Not ever seeing a friendly face
When every door seems to be firmly shut
And every wound is of the deepest cut

When our feelings cloak us in doubt
And we just can't figure it out
There seems to be no end to it all
We ready ourselves to take the fall

Maybe as a child you were at the mercy of others
Perhaps you have always felt isolated, so never ventured from under the covers
Years of torment that may have built up inside
Your optimism and hope long ago died

Those people who made you feel small
Took away everything, nothing left at all
Leaving you feeling empty, nothing left to give
Wanting to hurt them for forcing you to like this live

It does not require a vengeful act
Or for you to with yourself to make a pact
To hurt those people who took everything away
Making them for their actions pay

This will never make you feel complete
And never will it your demons beat
For two wrongs will never ever make a right
Using bitterness and hatred has never won a fight

Even if you saw the person fall
Turning a deaf ear when for you they called
The satisfaction would never last
In truth guilt would probably around you a shadow cast

If you wish to with yourself make amends
And start to with yourself be friends
Then a step in the right direction would simply be
To try and forgive, this will in the end set you free

Something amazing can then take place
Something can come along to fill the empty space
Just a small thought may start to formulate
Starting to erode away all of that hate

Sometimes you may wonder why
And if to yourself you are living a lie
But if you keep being strong and positive
You will eventually banish the negative

There will days when you will look back with a tear
But no longer will your memories fill you with fear
By forgiveness you will clearly see
That you are the one who has been set free

So next time you want to look back in hate
It is more harmful to you to be angry and yourself berate
Open your heart and learn to love yourself
Forgiveness after all is good for your health

To give with open heart and to freely love

Is a true gift from the Angels above

The Mist

I cannot see my hand in front of my face
I am lost and alone in this strange place
Everything seems to be obscured, I cannot see
Is there no one to hear my plea?

I came here, a question in my head
I need to listen closely to what is said
For sometimes I stumble upon the road I have been given
From my true purpose I often feel I have been driven

My future at the moment seems to be very bright
At last I am beginning to shine my light
But still I stumble and fall
And worry I won't hear your call

I don't want to get distracted from this pathway
Frightened I will get caught up and from it stray
I need to find you in this gloom
Need to see your face very soon

I know this is the mist of my mind
And you are there for me to find
I must see the pitfalls in front of my feet
See the way clear so you I can easily greet

My face I am no longer trying to hide
No longer so scared of what I will find
I am sure that in time as grow taller and taller
This mist will retreat the expanse becoming smaller

The day will come when I will see you on a daily basis
Yours and many other faces
I will recognize and greet with joy and love
For I know that my hand does indeed fit this particular glove

The Mist
©Shane Turnbull

Feeling Low

What do you do when you're feeling low?
Spread your sorrow wherever you go?
Or maybe you shut yourself away
Not emerge from your sorrow for many a day

Have you ever tried to picture yourself worse off than you are?
Think about others whom are worse off by far
Those whom for life is a battle beyond comprehension
Those who have little or nothing no love no attention

Some people who live with hardship day after day
Are beautiful souls and for others constantly pray
They never seem to feel sorry or moan about it all
They are often the ones who come running when you call

I wonder where they find the strength to carry on
Their hope never deserts them their faith never gone
Thinking of others before themselves all the time
Never winging or having a whine

I do not wish to imply your problem is not real
Or that at times how incredibly low we do feel
But sometimes a new perspective is all we need
You never know where it may lead

There will always be someone worse off than yourself
Whether it is in regard to money, relationship or health
So stop for a moment in the midst of your pain
And however difficult try to give thanks every now and again

For someone out there has to deal with so much more
Maybe they need some love to find the key to a new door
By spreading your love, hope and light however you feel
You will ensure that your life will run smoothly like a well-oiled wheel

Sure the odd puncture you may have to endure
But by helping others you will find the right cure
My love I send out to all who read this
And pray that you find peace, love and ever enduring happiness

The Road We Travel

I sit, I watch, I wait
I know you ponder upon the reality of fate
Do you really choose your own destiny?
If so is your will really free?

This question is asked over and over again
Yet the answer is always the same
Your choices were made before you came here
Not under duress or born out of fear

When you chose to once again visit this plane
You do so with excitement and joy at the lessons you will gain
Maybe you have chosen to come back to help another
Maybe your pain has something to teach your Earthly mother

It could be that you are part of a bigger plan
Many people comeback, sometimes to aid one man
Every Soul will have its place
No action ordered put to waste

So take heart in everything you do
Everyone you meet, no matter whom
Will have been put in your pathway
So that hopefully lessons will be learnt one day

Even the people that make you mad
Or seem to be nothing but bad
Will have a role to play in the web of life
Maybe *they* need to learn how to deal with strife

Every tear you cry, every impossible situation you're in
When the chips are down and you're certain you will never win
Somewhere in the black of the night
There will be the flicker of your light

I can only look back and wonder at how
I honestly thought I wouldn't be where I am now
But the pathway that I have trod with such difficulty
Has helped me grow into the person you see

Every mountain I have had to climb
(Sometimes it seemed to be three at a time)
I know where put there for me to scale to the top
Something inside made me never stop

Don't get me wrong my friends
I have had days where I needed it all to end
Wishing I would never ever again wake
My life like a bad dream crying enough tears to fill a lake

I am sure many of you have felt the same
But would I change it for an easy life, fortune or fame?
Occasionally I may laugh and say 'yes please'
A life without obstacles sounds fab to me

But honestly; no I wouldn't change a thing
Because with each lesson a new song I can sing
The person I am, the people you are
The road we have travelled, no matter how far

Will be the one that was intended for us
In this my friends you must trust
Even when it seems fate or free will are far away
They are part of you, with you night and day

Because we choose which way to walk
Whether it is wise for us to that person talk
These decisions can divert us from our destined pathway
But eventually our original plan will come back into play

Plough the field

Words are swirling around my mind
The ones I want I cannot seem to find
Some are dark and heavy others are happy and light
I am confused what am I meant to actually write

Quite suddenly a tear falls from my eye
I have unexpectedly started to cry
As my emotions soar from high to low
The words I need start to flow

My tears are for the children of our world
For the terrible situations into which they are hurled
Many know nothing but pain and sorrow
They see no hope for a brighter tomorrow

Born with a gun in their hand
And told they must fight for their land
Their minds are filled with such hate
To die with honour is their only fate

Or facing the horrors that war does manifest
And the loss of loved ones that leaves them bereft
Streets blown apart, reduced to rubble
Unhappiness often breeds nothing but unrest and trouble

For some the fight for survival is an emotional one
Trying to understand what they have done
Why the people who are meant to love them so
Seem to draw such pleasure from their pain and woe

Day after day being beaten or berated
Told over and over again how they are hated
Pushed into a corner, forced to carry out unimaginable deeds
Adults deaf to their pleas

Children born into famine and poverty
The likes of our supermarkets they will never see
To have a handful of rice a day
Is what they look to God for and pray

There are many more situations across our planet like this
I could take forever and ever to list
These children crying out in pain
Have very little to lose but everything to gain

How can I make a difference? I hear you say
Maybe it is up to us to show them there is another way
That not everything and everyone is the same
As a race we need to start playing a different game

Give the children who are angry and broken
Someone to shine the light and belief in the kind words being spoken
Show the starving that there is enough to share
Donate even a little to the poor, restoring faith that we all care

Turn darkness into a beautiful healing light
We must never give up on our children's plight
We can start to make a difference in their lives today
Plough the field and sow the seeds for tomorrow is another day

The Power of Thought

What good can my thoughts do?
I hear many people ask
By opening our hearts we can make life an easier task

When others are prominent in your mind
Whether for reasons good or bad
Open your heart and send them a thought of the healing kind

In times of trouble, when thoughts are dark and our tears do fall
We will beg and plead for help
Rest assured, spirit will always hear your call.

Meditation is a time when our thoughts can roam free
We can be transported to another place
Where only beauty you will see.

Don't limit your thoughts to those you know
Send healing across the world
Helping peace and harmony to grow

The thoughts of childhood, whether they be good or bad
They have the power to mould our lives
Making us feel happy or overwhelmingly sad.

Now let's use our power of thought, to reach out for that rainbow
Then as we dance upon the moon and catch a falling star
We can banish fear, allowing love to grow.

My Craggy Tree

Alone I don't wish to be
I am standing in the snow at the base of my craggy tree
Your branches reach out to shield me from the weather
You stand here leaving your post never

I often come here to think
The tranquillity clears my mind, brings me back from the brink
I often wrap my arms around the breadth of your trunk
You help me when my optimism is sunk

My mind I want to run free
I ask that you help and guide me
I can connect with your roots
I even feel their strength through my heavy boots

They are connected to Our Mother as am I
You help me to myself be true, enable me to fly
To see through the mess of my own making
Help me from this slumber awaken

I shall stay for just a little while longer
I now feel so much stronger
Even though the snow is on the ground
Inner warmth I have found

Thank you my wonderful friend
For the Healing energy you send
I am feeling so much better now
The frown has left my brow

I make my way across the field in which you stand
I stand and observe this beautiful snow covered land
Mother Nature you provide us with all we need
Sustenance, beauty and strength with which to carry out any given deed . . .

The Craggy Tree
©Shane Turnbull

What is Happening to the World Today?

What is happening to the world today?
Earthquakes, floods, unrest and war
I wish my footsteps took me a different way

I hate to see such suffering and pain
Hands reaching out for help
Everywhere I look, sickness, poverty and children whom are lame

The world is changing at an alarming speed
Vibrations shifting, moving around
Does this signify the beginning of the end of selfishness and greed?

This is how, as a race we have evolved
And we have to face the consequences of our actions
The problems we face need to be resolved

But seeing it all in front of me unfold
Even knowing what I know, leaves me feeling sad
Wanting to reach out and bring everyone in from the cold

This I know is all part of a bigger plan
For us to move forward and gain pace
A new and exciting direction for man

But knowing and understanding are two very different things
And trying to comprehend the suffering
Is difficult when I see the devastation change brings

But I must keep my head and understand
That the Great Spirit is all knowing
And it will all turned out as planned

In the meantime as a single person on my own
I cannot really hope to do much
But if I let my voice be heard, others will join in, I will not be alone

Together we can lift the vibration in harmony
Help others to understand and acknowledge
That this is the way forward, the way to be free

The fighting and turmoil that at the moment we have to endure
Is a means to an end,
A spoonful of bitter medicine will often cure

So join me as I send my healing ray
To all those suffering night and day
Let us join our hands and hearts
We all need to play our part
Then eventually when the time is right
And the vibrations are at the appropriate height
We can all glory in the wonder of what lies ahead
And listen adhering to what is being said
I am sure it will be something like this . . .
'Simply to love one another with open heart
And you will experience feelings of unparalleled bliss

Love

If you listen closely to spirit
This is what you will hear
The single most important thing is to love
We need to open our hearts and not live in fear

Many of us look at our lives
And often make judgement on others
We need to have more understanding
As we are all sisters and brothers

Some may find it hard
To live their life this way
But if we learn to love thy neighbour
We will find colour in our lives every day

We all have enough love to go around
It's an endless supply to share
So why not learn how to give and receive
Making the most of any opportunity to show we care

We should always listen to others
Even though we may not agree
We all have the right to our own opinion
The love in our heart will set our mind free

So together let's hold out both hands
Giving openly our love so pure
Then we can all as one embrace life
And allow love to be our cure

Hope

That one word can evoke such feeling
It can lift you up high enough to reach any ceiling
Fill your heart with beautiful song
Give you reason to want to right the wrongs

I see hope everywhere I look
I read it in the pages of many books
I see it when I walk down the street
I feel it in some of the people I meet

Hope is a child that has come in from the rain
Boldly stepping forward regardless of their pain
To make the world a better place to be
Help to understand that in order to love their heart needs to be free

Hope gives us a reason to get up and face the day
It can help us to hold our head up high, remove obstacles in the way
Filling us with a sense of purpose
Giving us reason to not always think the worst

Hope keeps the negativity at bay when all seems lost
Keeping the glimmer of light burning when our world has been turned and tossed
With our heart beating fast we take our first faltering step
It helps keep us strong when all our tears we have wept

Hope is what helps the world turn night and day
It encourages us to work together to find another way
When war is at its height and violence is the norm
Hope becomes a lifeline and takes on a very different form

For some hope is what makes their world a better place to be
And enables them to dream of the reality of being free
Putting a smile upon their face come rain or shine
Although they have little they never seem to whine

My heart goes out to those in desperate need
I cannot believe that upon deaf ears they often plead
Yet still I see that light that is eternally burning
Hope keeps at bay their desperate yearning

Hope is what the birds sing in their song
We can hear them all day long
Calling to each other in beautiful tune
Regardless of their size and beauty of their plume

Hope is what we always hear
When Spirit whisper in our ear
Hearing the gentle guidance they share
Encouraging us to show others we care

Think of a world without hope
What misery it would bring
Darkness would penetrate
Desperation would be king

Hope burns eternal, this is true
Even in your darkest hour let this apply to you
Don't ever let go of hope however bad it may seem
That dot on the horizon, that glint you can see, that is hope starting to gleam

All in a Day

What a difference a day makes
Sometimes just a change of direction is all it takes
A few words that can change your point of view
Allowing clear thinking of breaking through

Things are often not what they seem
The reality very different than the dream
A situation that seems dreadful one day
Can be rectified by the things we say

Confusion, pain and hurt
Senses blunted, not alert
Your Heart and Soul cry in pain
You are sure you will never feel the same

Stomach twisting and feeling sick
Head thumping, your thoughts foggy and thick
Sleep evades you no matter how tired you are
However fast you run, it isn't very far

Feelings such as these can cloud our mind
Making it almost impossible to see, leaving us blind
Common sense it seems has deserted you
Everything is black from this point of view

But as mentioned just before
Even when something has rocked us to the very core
A special place to clear your thoughts
Somewhere solace and contemplation can be sought

Can help drive the demons away
Making it easier for any words needed to say
And maybe when those words have been spoken
Something new inside will have awoken

It is strange how things can twist our mind
Situations, feelings getting us into a terrible bind
When the reality is oh so different in the cold light of day
Often it is to ourselves the heaviest price we pay

My special place is the sea
When I am there everything else ceases to be
With the wind in my hair and touching my face
I retreat inside to that special place

When I leave it seems to stay with me
Enabling my emotions to run free
Investigating what went wrong
Allowing me to think hard and long

So don't lose heart my dear friends
Even if you think a certain situation my never end
Open your heart and mind
And maybe the words needed you will find

For I have found out just these past few days
Felt so many emotions in so many ways
How things can be taken out of context
And I was left feeling angry and vexed

But had I looked closer, not shut myself away
I would have seen some very different emotions come into play
Lucky for me I was able to talk it through
Face my adversary and speak words that were true

In doing this act my thoughts turned around
And inner peace I have found
I was fortunate, forced to show my hand
But in doing so the stronger I stand

So when things are truly bad
And you feel angry, bitter and sad
Try to seek a place of solitude
A magical silent interlude

Be alone to explore how you feel
Then take action to make it real
Try to speak the words that need to be said
Stop them from filling your head

Yes it can take courage especially if never done before
But hopefully a suitable adversary will land at your door
Someone who is willing to hear what you have to say
Will listen to you come what may

My beating heart is now still
I have climbed a very steep hill
My view is now un obscured and clear
I can walk forward without fear

So speak out when something is amiss
Don't stand back and wish
For when we sit on our feelings, hide them away
We will never ever find our true pathway

Just For You

This poem is just for you
Every word needs to be listened to
How are you feeling today?
Are your skies blue or grey?

Where have you been?
What have you seen?
Has it been good or bad?
Has it made you feel happy or sad?

Do you feel lonely and low?
Maybe you have received a bitter blow
Do you want to hide away from every one?
Fighting a situation you feel will never be won

Lifting your head to the heavens you cry
The question on your lips is; why?
Is there ever anyone who hears your call?
Why is it you that always takes the fall?

Your voice is no longer heard even if you shout
This hole is so deep, will you ever get out?
Are you tired of fighting so hard?
You long to laugh, let down your guard

Knowing when to reach out
Can be a difficult task to take in hand
If you really want it the advice will always be there
Give people the opportunity and you will see that they really care

Try to unlock your frightened heart
Even the smallest step would be a good start
Only placing one foot in front of the other at a time
Feeling afraid will never be a crime

Sometimes finding another with common ground
Can feel like salvation has been found
Seeing that another has come through the other end
Can be the beginning of you starting to mend

As you face each new morn
Try not to see yourself as the pawn
Look in the mirror and smile at yourself
Tap into your untold inner wealth

Take a look at the world around
Only accept the beautiful sights and sounds
Try to block out anything that may hurt
Brush away any words that are curt

Take this advice and you should find
That you will slowly relax and unwind
The things that hurt and make you feel sad
Will gradually feel less and less bad

You may find that in time
You will be the one that feels fine
When you come across another feeling low
They may have taken a similar blow

It will be then that you will realize
And you will be able to see through their disguise
Reaching out the helping hand
Quietly letting them know that beside them you stand

At some point I am sure it will become clear
That through bravely facing your fear
You have in turn learnt how to help another in need
Seeing that good can grow from the tiniest seed

The pattern will repeat itself again and again
A cycle of healing and pain
But life, love and spirit go hand in hand
Showing us that things turn out just as planned

Change

The key to our future are the young
Yet for things to get brighter a new song has to be sung
A new direction for them needs to be found
Our teachings need to take on a different sound

When born into this life our Soul purpose is clear
Yet in a very short time this is lost due to fear
The adults around us unwittingly help us forget
Reminding us often of our earthly obligations to be met

To move forward we have a choice to make
A very wise and bold decision to take
As we help those young inquisitive minds to grow
It is up to us to help that light inside glow

Give them the tools they need every day in this life
Wise words will guide them away from trouble and strife
An open mind and heart will show them how to live
And what it truly means to give

Maybe a new way of teaching needs to unfold
These children are fed up of being told
They come with knowledge inside abound
Just waiting to be tapped into and found

Sitting at a desk hour after hour
Even to me; an adult is dour
Having to write page after page
Fractions, paragraphs and things from a different age

Some of those things they need to know
But if you really want a child's thoughts to flow
Then take them outside, the biggest classroom of all
Allow them to let nature to them call

Let them run free expanding their minds
Encourage them to investigate what they find
They will find the direction they need to take
And will discover about choices they may need to make

Reading and writing of course is an essential skill
But we don't need to go over kill
As a race we haven't realized the most important thing
We all have something different to the table to bring

If a child can't read or write
Maybe they have skill in another area ready to take flight
So what if little Jimmy can't sit still
Maybe he was born to discover; climb every hill

It is time to stop making every child fit into one mould
I am afraid that point of view is tired and old
I am sorry if my opinion grates against you
But you must understand this is a different point of view

As a mother I let my children grow
I will support them in whichever direction they decide to go
As long as they are good and true
And carry in their hearts the colour of every hue

I have one child who cannot read
For years the system has shown him he cannot succeed
But I will argue that point until the day I die
He is a beautiful person and has wings enough to fly

So he doesn't fit in to the slot that has been made
But never will I let his light fade
He has empathy that would put any adult to shame
And never have I heard him berate or lay blame

His heart is as huge as a house
But his self-confidence has been hammered down to the size of a mouse
This is what our society does if we 'don't fit in'
You seem to be discarded, thrown in the bin

Well I say it is time to change, so let us begin
With knowledge and understanding this fight we can win
The one thing that holds us back is fear
But if we let them the youth will make the way clear

The next generation is waiting to come in from the cold
So now it's our turn to be told
Allow them to learn about our Mother Earth
And teach them of love for each other and self-worth

Then we will have taken our part in shaping this place
Helping heal the wounds of our land and slowing the pace
Living our Soul Purpose and functioning as one
This has been the intention since time has begun

Freedom

What is freedom?
Does it mean we can roam free
Without constraint the world at our feet for us to see

Does freedom mean no life behind bars?
No tyrant to hold you under his boot
Not having to unwilling hold a gun and shoot?

Maybe to you financial freedom is what you crave
Not having to struggle day to day
Not having to worry about the bills you have to pay

Could it be you are trapped by circumstance?
Your wings have been clipped by something beyond your control
Feeling like you are down a deep dark hole

There are many things that hold us back
But to be truly free
All you have to do is open your eyes and see

Freedom is a state of mind
No matter where you are or what you do
Freedom can be an option for you

Up until recently I was trapped
Many things for me held me back
I despaired at the things I thought I lacked

However I have been on a journey
It took me to places in my mind
Many new things about myself I did find

I discovered something invaluable
That the freedom I so desperately longed for
Was there all the time locked behind a solid door

I met my Guide who I listened to intently
I was taught how to find the key
Walk forward and from the ties that bind be free

I am now free my mind has opened
I have this feeling inside of myself
I am rich beyond belief, filled with wealth
The lesson I have learned has changed my life
And for everyone this can be within reach
I now have something amazing to teach

Freedom that wonderful beautiful word
That can mean so much to one and all
Is waiting inside for you to call

I wish with all my heart
I could share with you the feelings it brings
My heart and soul now sing

Freedom brings with it the knowledge
That as a person you can achieve all that your heart desires
You just need to learn how to stoke the fires

I was told many years ago that for some
Being locked up against their will, nothing to gain
Or being trapped inside a body that knew nothing but pain

Even though hard, still this did not hinder their freedom
I found this difficult to believe
How can you gain when nothing do you receive?

But now I know their secret
Their mind knew freedom of the kind
Many people who walk this plane will never find

Now I have learnt my freedom
I understand that my life is totally in my hands
I am absolutely responsible for my future plans

I am who I am, I look the way I look
This is me, I love everything about who I am
I have faults, I am not posh or glam

Physical beauty has passed me by
My waist is a little too thick and bumpy
And yes sometimes I can be a tad grumpy!

But I have learnt my truth
I was born this way to show that variety is the spice of life
Why should what others say to me cause trouble and strife?
So my friends freedom can be found
Look inside your heart
This will be a good place to start

You hold the key to your very own truth
Seek your freedom it is there inside of you
All that has to be done is to yourself be true

As I hold my hand over my heart
I have but one wish for all of mankind
To find their freedom to leave self-hate behind

To love another completely you have to love yourself
In finding your freedom this will open doors
Bringing with it riches galore

I have spent many years in sad state
For myself held nothing but hate
Over and over again myself I did berate

Now I feel amazing reaching for new heights
Come join me on my journey of self-discovery
Don't turn away from my heartfelt plea

Learn to love exactly who you are
Keep the self-loathing at bay
For you are unique, amazing, special in every single way

Your footsteps toward freedom can start today
Time for a change see your life in a different light
For we are all beautiful, amazing beings of light

Christmas Seed

This Christmas I would like to bestow something upon you all
It is a gift, one that is very, very small
This gift I wish to share is the tiniest little seed
Warmth, food and light is all it will need

Before any harvest your seed you will have to sow
You possess everything inside of you to enable it to grow
You don't have to be magical, special or cast a spell
Listen carefully and to you the secret I shall tell

With these ingredients your seed will grow tall
Roots reaching down, providing foundation so it will not fall
Leaves and branches breaking through and reaching high
Why stop when the limit can be beyond the sky?

In no time at all your seed will become a tree
Swaying in the breeze alive and free
Nothing to stand in its way or hold it back
No one to hurt it or subject it to attack

This time next year when Christmas once again comes round
You can decorate your tree with the riches you have found
For upon every branch rests an abundance of special leaves
And each leaf holds universal love, healing and belief

Belief that if we all plant our special seed
Then from the restraint of fear we will be free
Can you imagine if everyone was handed such a gift
The light of love would penetrate enabling the fog to lift

My tree I feed every day, it's easy to maintain
By keeping my tree good and strong much I have to gain
For when I see it reaching out, branches laden with love
I know for sure it is also being fed from the Angels above

As I see the decorations glimmer and twinkle in the light
I stand back admiring the beautiful sight
I can visualize every bauble holds something very special indeed
It's filled with a million brand new seeds

I know as I wrapped every string of tinsel around my tree
Spirit were standing by my side helping me
Guiding me as they always do
Helping my heart and soul to be true

So next year when your tree is good and strong
We all know how time flies, so it won't be long
Make sure you laden it with gifts galore
You will multiply in the act of giving more

So once the food has been opened and presents unwrapped
When the TV is on and everyone is taking a nap
Try to remember your smallest gift of all
With the correct nourishment it will be mighty and tall

So as our loved ones past and present draw near
I would like to take this opportunity to wish you a peaceful Christmas
And a prosperous New Year
Please just give a thought to those on Christmas day
Who have nothing or no one
For even the smallest thought will go a long way

Moving On

As I turn to look one last time
The tears in my eyes shine
My footsteps echo in this lonely room
The Walls here no longer my tomb

As I reach for the door, I stumble
Time to walk in the sun, stop being so humble
Why has no-one ever heard my voice?
I have been shouting forever, I haven't had a choice

With courage in my heart I take it all in
Everything before me, it's grim
But as I focus my heavy eyes in the darkness
I see I have been walking my pathway, no more, no less

The room in which I stand although holds much pain
It also shows me, how by never giving up I have gained
Everything is played out before me
It's all there for me to see

Time to close the door on things past
Build upon what I have learnt, foundations that will last
The tools I have gained will never leave
They help me in my future, to never give up, to believe

Grasping the handle fear grips me
For what lay on the other side I cannot see
But something pushes me onward, my heart beating
I open the door, I close my eyes afraid of what I am meeting

The sun is warm upon my face
Still afraid to look I stand still getting the feel of this place
Joy fills my fragmented heart, healing the cracks
I begin to feel more complete, love for myself filling the gaps

Slowly my eyes open wide, they have a will of their own
I see that from my nest I have well and truly flown
No longer the fledgling that has held me back
My new feathers giving me the courage I did lack

I walk forward in my new world every day
Listening closely to what my head and heart say
Building upon that strong foundation that will forever be
I understand that the act of being trapped has now set me free

I still find the odd pot hole to fill
But my road stretches before glistening, my heart is still
No longer thumping in my chest
For I have figured out at last what for ME is best

To move forward we often have to leave something behind
Even though we may not see at the time that it is not cruel, but kind
The clouds will one day lift and all will be reviled
Our choices, the pathway we walk was long ago signed and sealed

So fear not, walk forward with courage in your heart
If your choices have seemed bad so far maybe it's time for a new start
Open your door, leave behind what before has gone
It's your time now, time to walk forward, time to move on . . .

Moving on
©Shane Turnbull

Let love be your guiding light

And the possibilities can be endless

Epilogue

I hope you have enjoyed reading **The Butterfly Fields** and that the poems on these pages have bought you comfort in troubled times, enlightenment and upliftment.

My journey up until now I have taken alone, but with you I would like to extend my journey. To take you even further, together we can discover new ground, unveil innermost thoughts, take joy from our successes learn from our mistakes and shine our light into the darkest corners.

My next book is in the process of being written and any comments or stories from you would be welcomed.

Please contact me at @CarolePilcher on Twitter or find me on facebook @ Carole Vickie Pilcher